THE NATURAL REPUBLIC

Reclaiming Islam from Within

"And let there be a nation from among you who calls towards goodness, and orders kindness, and prohibits evil. And these are the successful ones." (Qur'an 3:104)

The Monotheist Group

Brainbow Press
United States of America

The Natural Republic
Reclaiming Islam from Within
Copyright © 2010 by The Monotheist Group

Note: All translations of the Scripture used in this book are from "The Message – A Translation of the Glorious Qur'an (Second Edition)" by The Monotheist Group unless otherwise stated.

For information:
www.brainbowpress.com
www.free-minds.org
www.progressivemuslims.org

ISBN-13: 978-0-9796715-8-6
ISBN-10: 0-9796715-8-2

Printed in the United States of America

The work in these pages should not be considered to be divine and unchangeable. It is merely a human effort to try to find the best interpretation. The reader is asked to always *verify* and not readily accept the opinion of others as far as the subject of the words of God and His teachings are concerned.

> *"And do not uphold what you have no knowledge of. For the hearing, eyesight, and mind, all these you are responsible for." (Qur'an 17:36)*

To humanity…May we travel the 'Straight Path' together.

> *"And hold firmly to the rope of God, all of you, and do not be separated. And remember the blessing of God upon you when you were enemies and He united your hearts. Then you became, with His blessing, brothers; and you were on the edge of a pit of fire and He saved you from it; it is thus that God clarifies for you His signs that you may be guided." (Qur'an 3:103)*

CONTENTS

Preface

Many generations ago, Muslims used to lead the world in science, architecture, art, medicine, and, above all, justice. They used to be exemplary citizens and neighbors. They used to promote freedom of faith and freedom of expression at a time when all of Europe was mired in superstition and greed.

Then, things began to change. The Muslims themselves became less tolerant of other faiths, less tolerant of other opinions, and more susceptible to superstitions and worldly desires. The Muslims have been struggling with these problems well into the 21st century.

What has changed? What have Muslims changed that has caused this regression in their standing, their tolerance, and their adaptability? What have Muslims altered that has stopped their progress in science, medicine, and social justice?

Have the Muslims unknowingly broken the covenant of God and incurred His curse without even realizing it?

> *"As for those who break their pledge with God after having made its covenant, and they withhold what God has ordered to be delivered, and who cause corruption on the earth; upon those is a curse and they will have a miserable abode." (Qur'an 13:25)*

Modern Experimentation

Realizing that something somewhere had gone wrong, Muslims began to search for the older models of government that were in place during the time of the Prophet and the time of the companions shortly thereafter.

In Iran, we saw the 1979 revolution whereby the Shia experimented with the idea of an Islamic republic under the directives and leadership of the late Ayatollah Khomeini.

The governmental structure of Khomeini required that a group of the most learned clerics would use their study and knowledge of the Scripture and the Hadith to make executive decisions and to veto or pass laws. The Islamic state would have laws written by a parliament elected in multi-party elections around the country. This parliament would be made up of people from all walks of life, would be managed by a prime minister representing the majority party, and would be responsible for passing laws and making budgets. There would be an executive branch represented by a president. But exercising power over the parliament and the president would be a guardian council made up of the most learned and intelligent clerics. This guardian council would use the judicial principles of fiqh to determine whether laws were in accordance with Islam or were non-Islamic and whether certain measures (such as land reform) were properly Islamic or not. In addition, fiqh courts would replace all secular courts, and these fiqh courts, typically independent and decentralized, would all be organized under a supreme court, which would, like the courts, be a fiqh court.

The end result was a government that was enveloped in long bureaucratic and theological debates, yet made little movement forward towards the betterment of the lives of people. What also occurred was an increase in restrictions on the people who were expected to dress and behave in conformity with the moral views of the guardian council.

The Iranian experiment was deemed a failure as it did not meet the expectations of the Muslim masses and was not duplicated in any other region.

In 1996, we saw the Sunni attempt at a religious-based government whereby the Taliban emerged as a viable political power in Afghanistan, feeding dreams that an Islamic utopia could be established.

The Taliban government was established under the strict principles of Shariah law whereby its judges would rule in accordance with the Scripture, Sunnah, and opinions of the learned scholars. The Taliban model was a simple pyramid structure under which all legislative and executive power rested with the Amir Ul-Mumineen, who was, in this case, a man known by the name of Mullah Omar. The Taliban government structure severely restricted the lives of people, with women suffering the most, as they were forbidden from attending school or working outside their homes. And, they were publicly beaten if they were improperly dressed or escorted by men not related to them. The Taliban also made murder, adultery and drug dealing punishable by death and made theft punishable by the amputation of a hand. Men were required to grow their beards in emulation of the beloved Prophet Mohammed, and women were required to be covered from head to toe.

As with Iran, the Afghan experiment was deemed a failure with no other nation or people wanting to embrace the harsh and ruthless Taliban way of interpreting the Shariah. The Taliban dream was forever ended in late 2001 with a massive attack by the United States that decimated the government and its forces in a matter of days and left the Islamic world reeling from the blow suffered by the Sunni model (the stated reason for the attack was that Afghanistan was harboring Osama Bin Laden whom the US blamed for the 9/11 attacks).

The Alternatives

As a result of this failure to find a suitable system of government, the Islamic world has found itself embracing a number of different models of government in an effort to find what may be best for the concerned nation and its people. The current line-up of various systems/ governments includes:

- Autocracies: Saudi Arabia, Jordan, Egypt, Syria, Libya and the Gulf States are all governed either by a king or president who wields absolute power and authority.
- Democracies: Indonesia and Turkey are examples of states that have decided to manage their affairs by holding elections of the various officers of government.

Such governments have also experimented with a mix of social and economic models including, but not limited to: communism, capitalism, socialism, nationalism, etc.

Unfortunately, none of the above systems has provided the solution for the woes and problems of the Muslims. In fact, most of these systems have only added to their troubles, and the clearest proof of this is where we stand today.

Is There Hope?
After witnessing the inability of all Islamic nations that have emerged thus far to ameliorate the plight of Muslims, the burden now falls upon us to individually intervene and secure the future of our children.

Hope is at hand, and the answer to all our problems has always been right in front of us, yet we have been too distracted to pay attention.

Be warned that, as a Muslim, what you will read in this book will be disturbing to many of your established beliefs and that, to find the answers, we must face the truth about what we have become.

'The Natural Republic' that is described in this book and for which a constitution is provided is not being implemented anywhere at this moment in time. However, this does not have to be the case. If we are willing to put in some effort, we could give our children, and humanity in general, a better world to live in. Perhaps, The Natural Republic may be a viable model for post-war Iraq or Afghanistan. Or, it could be a solution for the Saudis or Egyptians who are growing dissatisfied with their current systems. Or, it could be a model for any nation in the world that is dissatisfied with the state of its affairs.

All we know for sure is that we will not progress unless we are willing to take the initiative.

> *"That is because God was not to change any blessing He bestowed upon a people, unless they change what is in themselves. God is Hearer, Knowledgeable."*
> *(Qur'an 8:53)*

This work is our initiative.
What will yours be?

The Monotheist Group
www.Free-Minds.Org
www.ProgressiveMuslims.Org

1

Why Do Muslims Lose?

Since at least the 1600s, the Muslims have been suffering from setbacks and losses, beginning with the military defeat of the Ottomans in Austria and the total collapse of the Ottoman Empire after World War I, to the Sykes-Picot agreement of 1916, the formal occupation of Palestine in 1948, the disastrous 1967 six-day war, and, more recently, the rapid collapse of the Taliban regime in 2001 and the defeat of the Iraqi regime in 2003.

The collapse of the Taliban regime in 2001 and the establishment of a US-backed government were very much predicted by all military and strategic analysts. The constant bombing by the United States destroyed whatever military the Taliban had and the psychological warfare had most of their troops ready to defect the first chance they got.

While a 21st century army defeating a 19th (or 20th) century army may have been as clear as day to many people, it came as an utter shock to most religious Muslims who could not understand how God, whom they believe in and worship, could abandon His people.

The Taliban were strict Sunni Muslims by the very definition of the word. They prayed five times a day and even offered the additional "extra credit" prayers as well. They grew their beards in emulation of the beloved Prophet, they dressed in the traditional dress of the 6th century Arabs, they banned television and cinema which cause evil and vice, they made their women cover themselves from head to toe to protect and honor this frail and sacred being, they had their women refrain from working and left them to look after the household thus helping them avoid evil and temptation which otherwise would have been their lot, they executed adulterous men and women in accordance with Shariah law, they cut off the hands of thieves in accordance with the same law, they taught their men to be strong and fight for the Shariah of God whenever they could, they destroyed statues that represented the blasphemous idols that people once worshipped alongside God...

In a nutshell, the Taliban were the textbook example of what a real Sunni Muslim society should be like.

Yet, the Taliban *lost!*

Did God not say in His glorious Book:

> *"God defends those who believe. God does not love any betrayer, rejecter." (Qur'an 22:38)*

"The ones who were driven out of their homes without justice, except that they said: "Our Lord is God!" And if it were not for God defending the people against themselves, then many places of gathering, and markets, and contact prayers, and temples where the name of God is frequently mentioned, would have been destroyed. God will give victory to those who support Him. God is Powerful, Noble." (Qur'an 22:40)

"And We have sent before you messengers to their people. So they came to them with clear proofs; then We took revenge on those who were criminals. And it is binding upon Us to grant victory to the believers." (Qur'an 30:47)

"O you who believe, if you support God, He will support you, and make your foothold firm." (Qur'an 47:7)

The verses above leave no doubt that God will support and grant victory to those who believe and serve Him.

Yet, the Taliban *lost!*

To the non-believers, the answer is clear: This was a matter of military might and of an advanced army fighting a primitive one!

To the Muslims, however, there is much more at stake. The Muslims know that God controls all actions and all matters, they know that God commands invisible and visible armies who come down to support His believers in times of need, they know that angels have been sent down in the past to support the Prophet in defeating his enemies (3:123), they know that a small and weak force can always defeat a larger and stronger force by the leave of God (2:249), they know that all the technology of the world, and all its power, and all its armies, are absolutely *nothing* when God is standing by the other party!

What the Muslims worldwide have on their hands is a true dilemma.

What has gone wrong?

Why has God abandoned them?

In nearly every single country and nearly every single place for many decades, the Muslims have been losing!

Have the Muslims broken their covenant with God?

- Do we need to pray more?

- Do we need to give more to charity?

- Do we need to grow our beards and cover our women (like Afghanistan)?

- Do we need to fast more days, or recite the Scripture more often at night?

What is it that the Muslims need to do?

A clue is found in the words of the Messenger himself:

> *"And the messenger said: 'My Lord, my people have deserted this Qur'an.' And it is so that We make for every prophet enemies from among the criminals. And your Lord suffices as a Guide and a Victor."* (Qur'an 25:30-31)

How is it that the Prophet will make this claim against us when there are over one billion Muslims on this planet who recite and read the Scripture day in and day out?

Do we not all teach our children to recite chapters from glorious Book of God?

How could it be said that we have deserted the Qur'an?

Abandoning the Scripture

It is not due to a lack of prayers, or the length of the beard, or the dress code of women that God has abandoned the Muslims. It has been because we have abandoned the word of God and have taken other paths and other gods besides Him without even realizing it.

God tells us that we are supposed to resort to His Book for judgment, yet we see Muslims time and time again resorting to their imams, or scholars, or leadership, or the Arab League, or the United Nations, or any other body except the one they were commanded to adhere to:

> "And We have sent down to you the Book with the truth, authenticating what is between your hands of the Book and superseding it. So judge between them by what God has sent down, and do not follow their desires from what has come to you of the truth. For each of you We have made laws, and a structure; and if God had willed, He would have made you all one nation, but He tests you with what He has given you; so strive to do good. To God you will return all of you, and He will inform you regarding that in which you dispute. And judge between them by what God has sent down, and do not follow their wishes, and beware lest they divert you away from some of what God has sent down to you. If they turn away, then know that God wants to inflict them with some of their sins; and many of the people are wicked. Is it the judgment of the days of ignorance that they seek? Who is better than God as a judge for a people who comprehend?" (Qur'an 5:48-50)

Even at the time of revelation, the disbelievers found the Scripture to be so detailed and meticulous that they pleaded with the Prophet, "Change it!"

> "And when Our clear revelations were recited to them, those who do not wish to meet Us said: 'Bring a Qur'an other than this, or change it!' Say: 'It is not for me to change it of my own accord, I merely follow what is inspired to me. I fear, if I disobeyed

*my Lord, the retribution of a great day!' Say: 'If God
had willed, I would not have recited it to you, nor
would you have known about it. I have been residing
among you for nearly a lifetime before this; do you
not comprehend?' Who is more wicked than he who
invents lies about God or denies His revelations? The
criminals will never succeed. And they serve besides
God what does not harm them or benefit them, and
they say: 'These are our intercessors with God.' Say:
'Are you informing God of what He does not know in
the heavens or the earth?' Be He glorified and exalted
above what they set up." (Qur'an 10:15-18)*

This is how the Scripture has been abandoned even
though it is being recited day and night. Its laws and
jurisdiction have been abandoned and whatever it says
about all walks of life has been ignored. The Muslims'
failure to adhere to the words of God starts at the very top,
i.e. with the structure of their governments, and trickles
down to their family structure, i.e. in how they treat
women and how they deal with their children, neighbors,
commerce, the environment, other religions, etc.

This is why the empire has ended and why we continue
to be defeated and humiliated throughout the world. We
have abandoned God, and God has thus abandoned us
and left us to our fate.

Is the Scripture Complete and Detailed?

God tells us that the Scripture is 'fully detailed' and
'complete' and a 'clarification for all things'.

*"'Shall I seek other than God as a judge when He has
sent down to you the Book fully detailed?' Those to
whom We have given the Book know it is sent down
from your Lord with the truth; so do not be of those
who have doubt." (Qur'an 6:114)*

"And the word of your Lord has been completed with the truth and justice; there is no changing His words. He is the Hearer, the Knower." (Qur'an 6:115)

"And the Day We send to every nation a witness against them from themselves, and We have brought you as a witness against these. And We have sent down to you the Book as a clarification for all things, and a guidance and a mercy and good tidings to those who have submitted." (Qur'an 16:89)

Yet, many Muslims still have doubts even after seeing all the evidence. They never dare question the Scripture openly, but they always find an excuse for why the Scripture cannot be followed on its own.

In Islam, there is no priesthood, and no religious hierarchy. However, as soon as you ask Muslims about their religion, they will refer you to the opinions of this or that Imam!

"And those who were weak will say to those who were mighty: 'No, it was your scheming night and day, when you commanded us to reject God and to set up equals to Him.' And they are filled with regret when they see the retribution — and We will place shackles around the necks of those who rejected. Are they not being requited for what they used to do? (Qur'an 34:33)

Perhaps, it is time for these people to realize just how dangerous their denial may be:

"These are the revelations of God, We recite them to you with the truth. So, in which narrative after God and His revelations do they believe? Woe to every sinful fabricator. He hears the revelations of God being recited to him, then he persists arrogantly, as if he never heard them. Give him news of a painful retribution. And if

he learns anything from Our revelations, he takes it in mockery. For these will be a humiliating retribution. Waiting for them is Hell. And that which they earned will not help them, nor those whom they have taken as allies besides God, and for them is a terrible retribution. This is a guidance. And those who reject the revelations of their Lord, for them is an affliction of a painful retribution." (Qur'an 45:6–11)

The Scripture is Easy to Understand

God tells us that the Scripture is clear to understand, and that any person who cares to understand it or learn from it will be given that understanding.

"And We made the Qur'an easy to remember. Are there any who want to learn?" (Qur'an 54:17)

Yet, the masses have refused to study the Scripture for themselves and insist on merely parroting its words, all the time leaving the so-called partners of God to do the understanding for them.

"And if they are told: 'Follow what God has sent down,' they say: 'No, we will follow what we found our fathers doing!' What if their fathers did not comprehend anything and were not guided? And the example of those who disbelieve is like one who repeats what he has heard of calls and cries; deaf, dumb, and blind, they do not comprehend." (Qur'an 2:170–171)

We are not surprised when we learn the Jews invented entire volumes of man-made books such as the Talmud and attributed them to God and His messenger (Moses). Nor are we surprised that Christians attribute a son to the Almighty! Yet, when anyone dares claim that Muslims have also been led astray through their own distortions, we are hit with waves of denial and shock, as we believe it is impossible that God would allow our religion to be altered.

Did God not say that He would permit those who have doubts in their hearts to be led astray?

> *"And as such, We have permitted the enemies of every prophet — human and Jinn devils — to inspire each other with fancy words in order to deceive. Had your Lord willed, they would not have done it. You shall disregard them and their fabrications. That is so the hearts of those who do not believe in the Hereafter will listen to it, and they will accept it, and they will take of it what they will." (Qur'an 6:112-113)*

The Great Disaster

By continuing along the path of denial and sectarianism, Muslims are risking more than just happiness and dignity in this world, for they also risk shame and retribution in the Hereafter...

> *"Those who had rejected will be told: 'The abhorrence of God towards you is greater than your abhorrence of yourselves, for you were invited to believe, but you chose to reject.' They will say: 'Our Lord, You have made us die twice, and You have given us life twice. Now we have confessed our sins. Is there any way out of this state?' This is because when God Alone was mentioned, you rejected, but when partners were set up with Him, you believed. Therefore, the judgment is for God, the Most High, the Great." (Qur'an 40:10-12)*

Unless we are willing to take the necessary steps to reform through self-examination and research, we will be led by our complacency and blind following of false idols into the abyss that is fast becoming our destination.

Are you content with what you already know?

> *"Then, when their messengers came to them with clear proofs, they were content with what they already had of knowledge. And they will be surrounded by that which they used to mock. So when they saw Our might, they said: 'We believe in God Alone, and we reject all the partners we used to set up!' But their belief could not help them once they saw Our might; such is the way of God that has been established for His servants; and the rejecters were then totally in loss." (Qur'an 40:83–85)*

God Alone

The true system of Islam, as revealed by God and His Messenger, has been neglected and ignored for many centuries by the Muslim masses while they blindly follow their scholars and leaders and their distorted and unauthorized teachings.

Muslims have been losing continuously because they have abandoned the word of God and replaced it with other laws and teachings which, in turn, has caused God to abandon them and leave them to their folly.

This life is not just about fun and games. It is about fulfilling our part of the pledge with God and proving that we can serve Him Alone.

> *"And when God Alone is mentioned, the hearts of those who do not believe in the Hereafter are filled with aversion; and when others are mentioned besides Him, they rejoice!" (Qur'an 39:45)*

Are we ready to embrace the path of God Alone and abandon all our idolatry?

Or, will we continue to lose?

2

The Enemies Within

As the Scripture was revealed, many people at the time were disturbed by its words, and they even pleaded with the Prophet to change the Scripture, but his answer was as clear as day:

> "And when Our clear revelations were recited to them, those who do not wish to meet Us said: 'Bring a Qur'an other than this, or change it!' Say: 'It is not for me to change it of my own accord, I merely follow what is inspired to me. I fear, if I disobeyed my Lord, the retribution of a great day!'" (Qur'an 10:15)

There were however a number of 'back doors' that these very same people later discovered: the unconditional love that people had for the Prophet and his family.

The two main sects that emerged in Islam, the Sunnis and the Shia, each had their own unique way of exploiting the system of God.

Back Door # 1—Hadith

The people who would lay the foundation of 'Sunnism' had found that people always wanted to hear about the life of the Prophet and what he used to say and do. In fact, this obsession can still be observed to this day when many Muslims speak for hours about the Prophet and his life, while they speak very little of God. It was thus that the door of Hadith (narrations) was opened whereby any saying or action could be attributed to the Prophet and would be automatically accepted as truth. What is even more disturbing is that, when a person who brought any Hadith was questioned about the content or authenticity of the saying, the crowd would react as if the Prophet himself was being insulted or as if his truthfulness was being questioned. Thus, the narrator of the Hadith miraculously became equal to the Prophet, and to question him was equated with questioning the Prophet himself!

History of Hadith

The word "Hadith" is inseparable from today's Sunni version of Islam and can best be translated as the sayings/narrations of the Prophet or his companions.

Hadith is promoted as the second source of Islam in Sunnism (the Scripture being the first) and has been well established as an entire science whereby people spend a lifetime merely studying the Hadith and its compilations.

The Sunnis teach that the Prophet brought the Scripture with him as well as his sayings ('Hadith') and actions ('Sunnah'). Hence, Sunni Muslims believe that these pillars are inseparable and that Islam cannot stand at all if any of these pillars is taken away.

What many of these staunch followers of the Hadith may fail to realize is that according to the available texts, the Hadiths did not begin to be recorded until nearly 60 years after the death of the Prophet, i.e. during the reign of Omar Bin Abdulaziz.[1]

In fact, according to the traditions, the grandfather of Omar Bin Abdulaziz (Omar Bin Al-Khatab) himself was supposedly vehemently opposed to the writing of any religious revelations except the Scripture:

> [Jami' Bayan Al-Ilm, Page 67] Omar Bin Al-Khatab is recorded as saying: "I wanted to write the traditions (Sun'an), and I remembered a people who were before you, they wrote other books to follow and abandoned the book of God. And I will never, I swear, replace God's book with anything."

Once the ban on Hadith was lifted, narrators began recording and gathering sayings and compilations related to the Prophet and his companions. There are countless stories of how this new pastime became an obsession for some narrators in that they would journey for hundreds of miles just to find one Hadith. The Hadith gathering and writing period continued for nearly 150 years after the lifting of the ban and today's most widely recognized Hadith collections are the following: Bukhari 870 A.D., Muslim 875 A.D., Abu Daud 888 A.D., Tirmidhi 883 A.D., Ibn Maja 886 A.D., and Al-Nisa'i 915 A.D.

In his opening statement, Bukhari (considered to be the first source of authentic Hadith) states that, out of nearly

---

1 The justification given by today's scholars for the 60-year ban is that the Prophet feared that the Hadith and Scripture would be intermingled into one book and this ban was simply a safeguard.

600,000 Hadiths known to him at the time, he could only record 7,397 as being authentically narrated by the Prophet. This is recognition by the collectors of Hadith that at least 98.76 percent of what people were attributing back to the Prophet was, at best, openly dubious!

Hadith Controversy

Bukhari and those who came after him spent countless years in the research and filtration of Hadiths until it became its own science. Bukhari relied upon the self-invented art of 'Transmission.' Thus, he states that a Hadith may be accepted as authentic or rejected as false based on who the Hadith comes from.

Bukhari made a study of the companions of the Prophet and established that the majority was trustworthy. He then asked about people who came after them, and, if the feedback appeared to be positive and credible, then Bukhari had no problem accepting a Hadith transmitted from that source.

To get over the obstacle of objectivity and the fact that Hadith was based mainly on hearsay, Bukhari found a very convenient Hadith (which Sunni scholars still quote) attributing super-human abilities to the companions of the Prophet and all Hadith narrators which enabled them to memorize word for word the sayings of the Prophet without any forgetfulness or distortion.

The irony here lies not only in the Hadith collection and recording, but, more importantly, in the outright *challenge* to the assertion of God that His Book is fully detailed and complete regarding all matters of faith and law that we require.

Even the choice of the word 'Hadith' is an act of defiance against God as He has said in His Book:

> *"These are the revelations of God, We recite them to you with the truth. So, in which narrative* (Hadith)

*after God and His revelations do they believe? Woe
to every sinful fabricator. He hears the revelations of
God being recited to him, then he persists arrogantly,
as if he never heard them. Give him news of a painful
retribution." (Qur'an 45:6–8)*

It is as if the Sunnis are answering the question of God
by saying, 'We believe in Bukhari and Muslim and Abu
Daud and Tirmidhi and Ibn Maja and Al-Nisa'i etc.'

Below is a small "sampling" of Hadiths[2] that Sunni
Muslims claim are a source of divine inspiration along
with the Scripture:

[Bukhari Volume 1, Book 9, Number 490:
Narrated Aisha] The things which annul the
prayers were mentioned before me. They said,
"Prayer is annulled by a dog, a donkey and a
woman (if they pass in front of the praying
people)." I said, "You have made us (i.e. women)
dogs. I saw the Prophet praying while I used to lie
in my bed between him and the Qibla. Whenever
I was in need of something, I would slip away. For
I disliked to face him."

[Bukhari, Volume 4, Book 54, Number 464:
Narrated Imran bin Husain] The Prophet said, "I
looked at Paradise and found poor people forming
the majority of its inhabitants; and I looked at
Hell and saw that the majority of its inhabitants
were women."

[Bukhari, Volume 3, Book 48, Number 826:
Narrated Abu Said Al-Khudri] The Prophet said,
"Isn't the witness of a woman equal to half of that

2 The full Hadith compilation can be read online at:
http://www.usc.edu/dept/MSA/fundamentals/hadithsunnah/

of a man?" The women said, "Yes." He said, "This is because of the deficiency of a woman's mind."

[Bukhari, Volume 4, Book 56, Number 829: Narrated Abdullah bin Umar] The Jews came to Allah's Apostle and told him that a man and a woman from amongst them had committed illegal sexual intercourse. Allah's Apostle said to them, "What do you find in the Torah (old Testament) about the legal punishment of Ar-Rajm (stoning)?" They replied, (But) we announce their crime and lash them." Abdullah bin Salam said, "You are telling a lie; Torah contains the order of Rajm." They brought and opened the Torah and one of them solaced his hand on the Verse of Rajm and read the verses preceding and following it. Abdullah bin Salam said to him, "Lift your hand." When he lifted his hand, the Verse of Rajm was written there. They said, "Muhammad has told the truth; the Torah has the Verse of Rajm. The Prophet then gave the order that both of them should be stoned to death. (Abdullah bin Umar said, "I saw the man leaning over the woman to shelter her from the stones.")

[Bukhari, Volume 1, Book 8, Number 387: Narrated Anas bin Malik] Allah's Apostle said, "I have been ordered to fight the people till they say: 'None has the right to be worshipped but Allah.' And if they say so, pray like our prayers, face our Qibla and slaughter as we slaughter, then their blood and property will be sacred to us and we will not interfere with them except legally and their reckoning will be with Allah."

[Bukhari, Volume 5, Book 58, Number 227: Narrated Abbas bin Malik]…Gabriel remarked, 'This is the Islamic religion which you and your followers are following.' Then the prayers were enjoined on me: They were fifty prayers a day. When I returned, I passed by Moses who asked (me), 'What have you been ordered to do?' I replied, 'I have been ordered to offer fifty prayers a day.' Moses said, 'Your followers cannot bear fifty prayers a day, and by Allah, I have tested people before you, and I have tried my level best with Bani Israel (in vain). Go back to your Lord and ask for reduction to lessen your followers burden.' So I went back, and Allah reduced ten prayers for me. Then again I came to Moses, but he repeated the same as he had said before. Then again I went back to Allah and He reduced ten more prayers. When I came back to Moses he said the same, I went back to Allah and He ordered me to observe ten prayers a day. When I came back to Moses, he repeated the same advice, so I went back to Allah and was ordered to observe five prayers a day.

[Bukhari, Volume 4, Book 54, Number 460: Narrated Abu Huraira] Allah's Apostle said, "If a husband calls his wife to his bed (i.e. to have sexual relation) and she refuses and causes him to sleep in anger, the angels will curse her till morning."

[Bukhari, Volume 4, Book 54, Number 540: Narrated Abdullah bin Umar] Allah's Apostle ordered that the dogs should be killed.

[Bukhari, Volume 4, Book 54, Number 539:

Narrated Abu Talha] The Prophet said, "angels do not enter a house witch has either a dog or a picture in it."

[Bukhari, Volume 4, Book 54, Number 509: Narrated Abu Huraira] The Prophet said, "Yawning is from Satan and if anyone of you yawns, he should check his yawning as much as possible, for if anyone of you (during the act of yawning) should say: 'Ha', Satan will laugh at him."

[Bukhari, Volume 4, Book 54, Number 513: Narrated Abu Qatada] The Prophet said, "A good dream is from Allah, and a bad or evil dream is from Satan; so if anyone of you has a bad dream of which he gets afraid, he should spit on his left side and should seek Refuge with Allah from its evil, for then it will not harm him."

[Bukhari, Volume 4, Book 54, Number 516: Narrated Abu Huraira] The Prophet said, "If anyone of you rouses from sleep and performs the ablution, he should wash his nose by putting water in it and then blowing it out thrice, because Satan has stayed in the upper part of his nose all the night."

[Bukhari, Volume 4, Book 54, Number 518: Narrated Ibn Umar] That he heard the Prophet delivering a sermon on the pulpit saying, "Kill snakes and kill Dhu-at-Tufyatain (i.e. a snake with two white lines on its back) and Abtar (i.e. a snake with short or mutilated tail) for they destroy the sight of one's eyes and bring about abortion." (Abdullah bin Umar further added): Once while I was chasing a snake in order, to kill it, Abu Lubaba called me saying: "Don't kill it," I said. "Allah's Apostle ordered us to kill snakes." He said, "But later on he prohibited the killing of snakes living in the houses." (Az-Zubri said. "Such snakes are called Al-Awamir.")

[Bukhari, Volume 4, Book 54, Number 522: Narrated Abu Huraira] The Prophet said, "When you hear the crowing of cocks, ask for Allah's Blessings for (their crowing indicates that) they have seen an angel. And when you hear the braying of donkeys, seek Refuge with Allah from Satan for (their braying indicates) that they have seen a Satan."

[Bukhari, Volume 4, Book 56, Number 841: Narrated Abu Huraira] I said, "O Allah's Apostle! I hear many narrations from you but I forget them." He said, "Spread your covering sheet." I spread my sheet and he moved both his hands as if scooping something and emptied them in the sheet and said, "Wrap it." I wrapped it round my body, and since then I have never forgotten a single Hadith.

[Bukhari, Volume 4, Book 54, Number 524: Narrated Abu Huraira] The Prophet said, "A group of Israelites were lost. Nobody knows what they did. But I do not see them except that they were cursed and changed into rats, for if you put the milk of a she-camel in front of a rat, it will not drink it, but if the milk of a sheep is put in front

19

of it, it will drink it." I told this to Ka'b who asked me, "Did you hear it from the Prophet ?" I said, "Yes." Ka'b asked me the same question several times.; I said to Ka'b. "Do I read the Torah? (i.e. I tell you this from the Prophet.)"

[Bukhari, Volume 4, Book 54, Number 525: Narrated Aisha] The Prophet called the Salamander, a mischief-doer. I have not heard him ordering that it should be killed. Saad bin Waqqas claims that the Prophet ordered that it should be killed.

[Muslim, Book 008, Number 3371] Abu Sirma said to Abu Sa'id al Khadri (Allah he pleased with him): O Abu Sa'id, did you hear Allah's Messenger (may peace be upon him) mentioning al-'azl? He said: Yes, and added: We went out with Allah's Messenger (may peace be upon him) on the expedition to the Bi'l-Mustaliq and took captive some excellent Arab women; and we desired them, for we were suffering from the absence of our wives, (but at the same time) we also desired ransom for them. So we decided to have sexual intercourse with them but by observing 'azl (Withdrawing the male sexual organ before emission of semen to avoid-conception). But we said: We are doing an act whereas Allah's Messenger is amongst us; why not ask him? So we asked Allah's Messenger (may peace be upon him), and he said: It does not matter if you do not do it, for every soul that is to be born up to the Day of Resurrection will be born.

[Muslim, Book 030, Number 5839] Abu Huraira reported Allah's Messenger (may peace be upon him) as saying: The crying of the child (starts) when the satan begins to prick him.

[Bukhari, Volume 2, Book 23, Number 423: Narrated Abu Huraira] The angel of death was sent to Moses and when he went to him, Moses slapped him severely, spoiling one of his eyes. The angel went back to his Lord, and said, "You sent me to a slave who does not want to die." Allah restored his eye and said, "Go back and tell him (i.e. Moses) to place his hand over the back of an ox, for he will be allowed to live for a number of years equal to the number of hairs coming under his hand." (So the angel came to him and told him the same). Then Moses asked, "O my Lord! What will be then?" He said, "Death will be then." He said, "(Let it be) now." He asked Allah that He bring him near the Sacred Land at a distance of a stone's throw. Allah's Apostle (p.b.u.h) said, "Were I there I would show you the grave of Moses by the way near the red sand hill."

[Bukhari Volume 5, Book 57, Number 15: Narrated Abu Huraira] I heard Allah's Apostle saying, "While a shepherd was amongst his sheep, a wolf attacked them and took away one sheep. When the shepherd chased the wolf, the wolf turned towards him and said, 'Who will be its guard on the day of wild animals when nobody except I will be its shepherd.' And while a man was driving a cow with a load on it, it turned towards him and spoke to him saying, 'I have not been created for this purpose, but for plowing.' The people said, "Glorified be Allah." The Prophet said, "But I believe in it and so does Abu Bakr and Umar."

[Bukhari Volume 5, Book 58, Number 188: Narrated Amr bin Maimun] During the pre-Islamic period of ignorance I saw a she-monkey surrounded by a number of monkeys. They were all stoning it, because it had committed illegal sexual intercourse. I too, stoned it along with them.

[Bukhari Volume 4, Book 54, Number 528: Narrated Aisha] The Prophet ordered that a short-tailed or mutilated-tailed snake (i.e. Abtar) should be killed, for it blinds the on-looker and causes abortion."

[Bukhari Volume 4, Book 54, Number 492: Narrated Abdullah] It was mentioned before the Prophet that there was a man who slept the night till morning (after sunrise). The Prophet said, "He is a man in whose ears (or ear) Satan had urinated."

[Bukhari Volume 4, Book 54, Number 505: Narrated by Abu Huraira] The Prophet said, "When the call for the prayer is pronounced, Satan takes to his heels, passing wind with noise, When the call for the prayer is finished, he comes back. And when the Iqama is pronounced, he again takes to his heels, and after its completion, he returns again to interfere between the (praying) person and his heart, saying to him. 'Remember this or that thing.' till the person forgets whether he has offered three or four Rakat: so if one forgets whether he has prayed three or four Rak'at, he should perform two prostrations of Sahu (i.e. forgetfulness)."

[Malik's Muwatta Book 49, Number 49.4.6] Yahya related to me from Malik from Ibn Shihab from Abu Bakr ibn Ubaydullah ibn Abdullah ibn Umar from Abdullah ibn Umar that the Messenger of Allah, may Allah bless him and grant him peace, said, "When you eat, eat with your right hand and drink with your right hand. Shaytan eats with his left hand and drinks with his left hand."

[Bukhari Volume 1, Book 6, Number 299: Narrated Abdur-Rahman bin Al-Aswad] (on the authority of his father) Aisha said: "Whenever Allah's Apostle wanted to fondle anyone of us during her periods (menses), he used to order her to put on an Izar and start fondling her." Aisha added, "None of you could control his sexual desires as the Prophet could."

[Bukhari, Vol. 1, Book 11, Number 626: Narrated Abu Huraira] The Prophet said, "No prayer is harder for the hypocrites than the Fajr and the 'Isha' prayers and if they knew the reward for these prayers at their respective times, they would certainly present themselves (in the mosques) even if they had to crawl." The Prophet added, "Certainly I decided to order the Mu'adh-dhin (call-maker) to pronounce Iqama and order a man to lead the prayer and then take a fire flame to burn all those who had not left their houses so far for the prayer along with their houses."

[Bukhari, Volume 1, Book 4, Number 215: Narrated Ibn 'Abbas] Once the Prophet, while passing through one of the grave-yards of Medina or Mecca heard the voices of two persons who were being tortured in their graves. The Prophet said, "These two persons are being tortured not for a major sin (to avoid)." The Prophet then added, "Yes! (they are being tortured for a major sin). Indeed, one of them never saved himself from being soiled with his urine while the other used to go about with calumnies (to make enmity between friends). The Prophet then asked for a green leaf of a date-palm tree, broke it into two pieces and put one on each grave. On being asked why he had done so, he replied, "I hope that their torture might be lessened, till these get dried."

Consequences of Hadith

God has created human beings with the natural tendency to be inquisitive. Anyone who has children will know that no matter how many times you tell them "No," they will still try to touch a hot pan or play with the dirt to understand why they should not do so. This is a God-given mechanism that our Lord has bestowed on the human species to let us expand our knowledge and only accept what we understand and know.

When Muslims were ruling and living by the Scripture, there was no problem as far as this natural human curiosity was concerned since the Scripture had an answer to every question. Muslims, at that time, witnessed an intellectual growth unparalleled in the history of Arabia or even the world.

The tendency to question and inquire led Muslim children to mature in an atmosphere where no kind of knowledge was off limits and nothing was taboo. Their questioning simply developed an unlimited appetite for information which was fed by discoveries and advancements in just about every field.

Then, a few hundred years after the Scripture had fueled this intellectual revolution in Muslim minds, something began to change.

The widespread introduction of Hadith and its popularity with the masses began to slowly create problems in the education of Muslims. Hadith could not compare to the Scripture due to its inferior language and its reliance on hearsay and conjecture.

We can only assume that the establishment of the Hadiths as a source of Islamic law was achieved many centuries after its initial gathering by having it forced on the Muslim masses and without tolerating scrutiny or questioning of it.

Muslim school children today are taught from a very early age not to question or overanalyze their sources of religion, as they might incur the wrath of God and walk the path to Hell in doing so.

Students' questions are typically answered with statements like "Are you better than the companions of the Prophet or previous generations?" Or, "Do you hate the Prophet so much that you question his words (Sunnah)?"

With such a barrage of accusations, young Muslim students learn early on to simply accept what they are told without thought or questions. And, when they are older, they simply repeat to the younger generation what was told to them about going to Hell and disrespecting the Prophet. The cycle continues!

However, the truth remains that the very same people who were dissatisfied with the Scripture when it was revealed managed to get their way in the end and to transform Islam into no more than a shell of its former self by creating new laws and rules that were designed to undermine the system the Scripture had brought, and to quell intellectual growth and development which is almost always the enemy of corruption, greed and disregard for justice and equality.

Back Door # 2—Ahlul Bayt

The group that would lay the foundation for 'Shiaism' took a slightly different approach from the Sunnis to undermine the Qur'an. These people claimed that the knowledge and wisdom of the Prophet did not end with his death, but was transmitted to his descendents ('Ahlul Bayt,') via Ali Bin Abi Taleb (the cousin of the Prophet), and that such people would be the bearers of all of the knowledge of the Prophet until Judgment Day.

According to mainstream Shiaism (The "Twelver" Shiites) there have been twelve Imams who have succeeded the Prophet Muhammad directly. These are:

1. Ali Bin Abi Taleb (d.661)
2. Al-Hasan (d.670)
3. Al-Husayn (d.680)
4. Ali Zayn Aal-'Abidin (d.713)
5. Muhammad Al-Baqir (d.733)
6. Ja'far Al-Sadiq (d.765)
7. Musa Al-Kazim (d.799)
8. Ali Al-Rida (d.818)
9. Muhammad Al-Jawad (d.835)
10. Ali Al-Hadi (d.868)
11. Al-Hasan Al-Askari (d.874)
12. Muhammad Al-Mahdi (still alive according to the Shia, but in hiding for over 1,000 years!)

The other descendants of Ali are still 'Ahlul Bayt,' but they are not of the same degree of holiness as the 'Special Twelve.' In fact, in places like Iraq, Iran and Lebanon, the recognition of a Shia who is from the 'Ahlul Bayt' is very simple as they will don a black turban signifying their elite status (Shia scholars who are not from the 'Ahlul Bayt' will don a white turban).

The Shia have also created a hierarchy of scholars who are ranked as per the following: Preacher, Mujtahid, Hujjat Al-Islam [Proof of Islam], Hujjat Al-Islam wa Al-Muslimeen, Ayatollah, and the great Ayatollah or Ayatollah Uzma. The higher the rank, the more powerful is the ability to pass binding laws (Ayatollah literally means a miracle or sign of God).

No Male Descendants for Mohammed
God has decreed that the prophethood and the Scripture would be retained exclusively within the progeny of Abraham:

> *"And We granted him Isaac and Jacob, and We made within his progeny the prophethood and the Book. And We gave him his reward in this world, and in the Hereafter he is among the righteous." (Qur'an 29:27)*

Under such a system, the progeny is passed on through the male or female heirs (as with Mary the descendent of Aaron), with the name retention being kept through the males only:

> *"Name them by their fathers. That is more just with God. But if you do not know their fathers, then, name them as your brothers in the system and your patrons. There is no sin upon you for what mistake you make in this respect; but you will be responsible for what your hearts deliberately intend. God is Forgiver, Merciful." (Qur'an 33:5)*

With regards to the Prophet Mohammed, God, in His infinite wisdom, has told us that the Prophet would not be survived by any males:

> *"Mohammed is not the father of any of your men, but he is the messenger of God and the seal of the prophets. And God is fully aware of all things." (Qur'an 33:40)*

Therefore, with only female descendants, the chain of the progeny is considered "weakened" in the traditionalist view. Thus, a plan was devised by the Shia sect to recreate the facts and give themselves access to a direct male progeny.

Cousin of the Prophet—Ali Bin Abi Taleb

The way the Shia had circumvented the physical restriction of God (whereby the Prophet did not leave any male descendants) was twofold.

Firstly, the Shia scholars referred to a verse in the Qur'an that speaks of God purifying the 'members of the family' (Ahlul Bayt) and thus giving them special status:

> *[Yusuf Ali Translation 33:33]: And stay quietly in your houses, and make not a dazzling display, like that of the former Times of Ignorance; and establish regular Prayer, and give regular Charity; and obey Allah and His Messenger. And Allah only wishes to remove all abomination from you, ye members of the Family, and to make you pure and spotless.*

While the above verse clearly does not mention Ali or his children, the Shia scholars simply dipped into the world of 'Hadith' where, lo and behold, Ali and his children are defined by the Prophet as 'Ahlul Bayt!'

> [Sahih Muslim, Chapter of virtues of companions, v4, p1883, Tradition #61] Narrated Aisha: One day the Prophet came out in the afternoon wearing a black cloak (upper garment or gown;

long coat), then Al-Hasan Ibn Ali came and the
Prophet accommodated him under the cloak,
then al-Husain came and entered the cloak, then
Fatimah came and the Prophet entered her under
the cloak, then Ali came and the Prophet entered
him to the cloak as well. Then the Prophet
recited: "Verily Allah intends to keep off from
you every kind of uncleanness O' People of the
House (Ahlul-Bayt), and purify you a perfect
purification" (the last sentence of Verse 33:33).

Secondly, the Shia scholars delved again into the
books of Hadith to prove that the mantle of authority
was indeed passed directly from the Prophet himself to
Ali bin Abi Talib:

[Nur al-Din al-Halabi al-Shafi'i, al-Sirah al-
Halabiyya, vol. 3, p. 337; Al-Zurqani, Sharh al-
Mawahib al-Ladunniyya, vol. 7, p. 13] When
the Prophet (s) was passing by this place on 18
Dhu'l Hijja (10 March 632) on his return from
the Farewell Pilgrimage, the verse "O Messenger,
Proclaim what has been sent down..." was revealed.
He therefore stopped to make an announcement to
the pilgrims who accompanied him from Makkah
and who were to disperse from that junction to their
respective destinations. By the orders of the Prophet
(s), a special pulpit made of the branches of trees was
erected for him. After the noon prayer the Prophet (s)
sat on the pulpit and made his last public address to
the largest gathering before his death three months
later. The highlight of his sermon was when, taking
Imam Ali (a) by the hand, the Prophet (s) asked his
followers whether he was superior in authority (awla)
to the believers themselves. The crowd cried out in
one voice: "It is so, O Apostle of Allah". He then

declared: "He of whom I am the master (mawla), of him 'Ali is also the master (mawla). O God, be the friend of him who is his friend, and be the enemy of him who is his enemy." Immediately after the Prophet (s) finished his speech, the following verse of the Qur'an was revealed: "Today I have perfected your religion and completed my favor upon you, and I was satisfied that Islam be your religion." (Qur'an 5:3) After his speech, the Prophet (s) asked everybody to give the oath of allegiance to Ali (a) and congratulate him. Among those who did so was Umar bin al-Khattab, who said: "Well done Ibn Abi Talib! Today you became the master of all believing men and women." An Arab, having heard of the event of Ghadir Khumm, came up to the Prophet (s) and said: "You commanded us to testify that there is no deity but Allah and that you are the Messenger of Allah. We obeyed you. You ordered us to perform the prayers five times a day and we obeyed. You ordered us to fast during the month of Ramadhan and we obeyed. Then you commanded us to make the pilgrimage to Makkah and we obeyed. But you are not satisfied with all this and you have raised your cousin by your hand and imposed him upon us as our master by saying 'Ali is the mawla of whom I am mawla.' Is this imposition from Allah or from you?" The Prophet (s) said: "By Allah who is the only deity! This is from Allah, the Mighty and the Glorious."

Of course, other than the fact that the Shia have resorted to the Hadith to make this claim, they have also spurned the Qur'anic truth which has defined for us who the 'Ahlul Bayt' are and what system of leadership/government we are to follow:

1. The 'Ahlul Bayt' are the guardians of the Restricted Sanctuary of Pilgrimage.

"And his wife was standing, so she laughed when We gave her the good news of Isaac, and after Isaac, Jacob. She said: 'O my! How can I give birth when I am an old woman, and here is my husband an old man? This is indeed a strange thing!' They said: 'Do you wonder at the decree of God? The mercy of God and blessings are upon you O people of the Sanctuary (Ahlul Bayt). *He is Praiseworthy, Glorious.'" (Qur'an 11:71-73)*

"You shall settle down in your homes, and do not go about like in the old days of ignorance. You shall hold the contact prayer, and contribute towards purification, and obey God and His messenger. God wishes to remove any affliction from you, O people of the Sanctuary (Ahlul Bayt), *and to purify you completely." (Qur'an 33:33)*

Here we have as clear as day God using exactly the same words when referring to Abraham as when he refers to Mohammed. Obviously this has nothing to do with Ali or Fatima as the Hadith stories narrate, but rather it has to do with a description of a people who are responsible for the sanctuary of God and have become its caretakers.

2. Government is through consultation, not succession.

"And those who have responded to their Lord, and they hold the contact prayer, and their affairs are conducted by mutual consultation among themselves, and from Our provisions to them they give." (Qur'an 42:38)

"It was a mercy from God that you were soft towards them; had you been harsh and mean hearted, they would have dispersed from you; so pardon them and

ask forgiveness for them, and consult them in the matter; but when you are convinced, then put your trust in God; for God loves those who put their trust."
(Qur'an 3:159)

God has given us guidance for how our affairs are to be conducted i.e. leadership based on open discussions and consultations rather than individual opinions and decisions. As such, the entire concept of inherited authority that the Shia base their beliefs on is in clear violation of the laws of the Qur'an.

Why Would God Allow This to Happen?

While Muslims have no problem accepting that the Jews and Christians and just about everyone else may have been diverted from the pure message of God Alone, they do have a problem in acknowledging that they have fallen into the same trap. Muslims will say things like "God has protected Islam," and "Islam has been this same way for centuries." They do not realize that these are the same arguments uttered by Jews and Christians when they are confronted about their beliefs!

The sad truth is that Muslims are just as human and just as vulnerable as everyone else. We do not have a magic talisman or superhuman powers that protect us anymore than the next person. We are frail and human and susceptible to suggestions and diversions just like everyone else.

In fact, had we been paying attention to the words of God rather than our scholars' opinions, we would have noticed that it is the decree of God that people who do not pay attention be misled:

"And as such, We have permitted the enemies of every prophet — human and Jinn devils — to inspire each other with fancy words in order to deceive. Had your

Lord willed, they would not have done it. You shall disregard them and their fabrications. That is so the hearts of those who do not believe in the Hereafter will listen to it, and they will accept it, and they will take of it what they will." (Qur'an 6:112-113)

This is about testing our belief and seeing whether we truly and actually believe in God and put our faith in Him, or whether we harbor inner doubts and therefore need to cling to human words and opinions.

It is about the test… God Alone, or God Plus?

3

Obey God and Obey the Messenger

In confronting the Sunni and Shia sects, who claim to be affiliated with the great system of submission to God, the topic that most comes up is the one about "obeying God and obeying the messenger."

While the sects reluctantly acknowledge that the Qur'an is fully detailed and complete as God has said it is (see 6:114-115, 11:1, 16:89), they quickly point to the many verses in the Quran which speak of "obeying God and obeying the messenger" and point out that such verses clearly mean there are two sources of information to be followed: "Obey God" meaning the Qur'an, and "Obey the Messenger" meaning the Hadith.

> *"And obey God and obey the messenger, and be aware. If you turn away then know that it is the duty of the messenger to deliver clearly." (Qur'an 5:92)*

> *"O you who believe, obey God and His messenger, and do not turn away from him while you have heard." (Qur'an 8:20)*

> *"O you who believe, obey God, and obey the messenger. And do not render your works in vain." (Qur'an 47:33)*

> *"Obey God and obey the messenger. And if you turn away, then it is only required of Our messenger to deliver clearly." (Qur'an 64:12)*

At first glance, the argument of the sects seems somewhat convincing, for surely if God had meant for us to simply follow the Qur'an He would have only said "obey God" and that would have been sufficient. However, by adding "and obey the messenger," the claim seems to have some support.

In verse 4:59 we see the case for the Sunnis and Shia further strengthened as the believers are told to "obey God" and "obey the messenger" and "obey those in authority" (seems to be three separate entities), however, if they dispute in any matter they shall ignore the opinion of "those in authority" and simply revert back to God and His messenger:

> *"O you who believe, obey God and obey the messenger, and those in authority among you. But if you dispute*

in any matter, then you shall refer it to God and His messenger if you believe in God and the Last Day. That is better and more suitable for knowing." (Qur'an 4:59)

What has been presented thus far is the logic used in justifying the opening of Pandora's Box where the definition of "what" the messenger delivered becomes a treasure hunt through the hundreds of thousands of old wives' tales and stories all attributed to the messenger doing or saying something.

What Did the Messenger Judge By?

Before putting an end to this controversy, it is worth noting that the Prophet himself was required by the Scripture to judge using the book of God and nothing but the book:

"We have revealed to you the Book with the truth that you may judge between the people by that which God has shown you, and do not be an advocate for the treacherous." (Qur'an 4:105)

"And We have sent down to you the Book with the truth, authenticating what is between your hands of the Book and superseding it. So judge between them by what God has sent down, and do not follow their desires from what has come to you of the truth. For each of you We have made laws, and a structure; and if God had willed, He would have made you all one nation, but He tests you with what He has given you; so strive to do good. To God you will return all of you, and He will inform you regarding that in which you dispute." (Qur'an 5:48)

"And the Day We send to every nation a witness And

the Day We send to every nation a witness against
them from themselves, and We have brought you as
a witness against these. And We have sent down to
you the Book as a clarification for all things, and a
guidance and a mercy and good tidings to those who
have submitted." (Qur'an 16:89)

So, how can a man who was commanded to judge and live according to the Qur'an be able to produce anything external to the Qur'an?

Obey God and Obey the Messenger

The answer to this entire issue is found once again in the Qur'an itself:

"Whoever obeys the messenger has obeyed God; and
whoever turns away, We have not sent you as a
guardian over them." (Qur'an 4:80)

While this may come as a shock to the sects, it is a natural answer for students of Qur'an who know and believe the word of God to be detailed and complete. We are told in no uncertain terms that whoever has "obeyed the messenger" has automatically met the requirement of "obeying God" (i.e. the two commands are one and the same).

A little thought by the sects would have led them to the same conclusion, for, after all, the Qur'an was never revealed to us by God directly, but was done through His inspiration to His messenger (i.e. the messenger, God, and the Qur'an are inseparable).

It was not left to the companions of the Prophet or any other people to come along and complete the religion for us. The religion was complete on the day God said it was so:

"...Today I have perfected your system for you, and
completed My blessings upon you, and I have approved

37

submission as the system for you…" (Qur'an 5:3)

There is no external text to be sought; no Hadiths… There are only the words that the messenger delivered while being inspired by God.

> *"Say: 'Which is the greatest testimony?' Say: 'God is witness between me and you, and He has inspired to me this Qur'an that I may warn you with it and whoever it reaches, that you are bearing witness that with God are other gods!' Say: 'I do not bear witness!' Say: 'He is only One god, and I am innocent of what you have set up!'" (Qur'an 6:19)*

Is the Messenger a Mere Postman?

Unfortunately, the sects will continue to believe that somehow it is not enough that the Prophet would only deliver the Scripture (even if it contained all those words revealed to him by God). They want the Prophet to do much more, perhaps even more than raising the dead as Jesus did or splitting the sea as Moses had done!

Perhaps such people are not far descended from those before them who also were not satisfied with the Qur'an and asked the Prophet to change it altogether for them.

> *"And when Our clear revelations were recited to them, those who do not wish to meet Us said: 'Bring a Qur'an other than this, or change it!' Say: 'It is not for me to change it of my own accord, I merely follow what is inspired to me. I fear, if I disobeyed my Lord, the retribution of a great day!'" (Qur'an 10:15)*

Of course, the sensible ones know that delivering the word of God, and being a living example of the message, is more than enough honor for any creature in this universe and beyond.

> *"Had We sent down this Qur'an to a mountain, you would have seen it trembling, crumbling, out of concern from God. And such are the examples We put forth for the people, that they may reflect." (Qur'an 59:21)*

Why Send a Messenger?

Here is the major question that people face when discussing the following of the Qur'an alone—why send a messenger? Surely, some would argue, God could have just delivered a completed Book and saved everyone the problems and arguments and misunderstandings.

The truth is those who were bound to reject the word of God would reject it no matter what:

> *"And if We had sent down to you a book already written on paper, and they touched it with their own hands, then those who have rejected would say: 'This is but clear magic!'" (Qur'an 6:7)*

As for the messenger, his duty was, as other messengers before him, to deliver the clear message of God and warn of the inevitable day when all would stand humbled before God:

> *"Say: 'I am no different from the other messengers, nor do I know what will happen to me or to you. I only follow what is inspired to me. I am no more than a clear warner.'" (Qur'an 46:9)*

> *"And thus We have inspired to you an Arabic Qur'an, so that you may warn the capital town and all around it, and to warn about the Day of Gathering that is inevitable. A group will be in the Paradise, and a group in Hell." (Qur'an 42:7)*

The Example of the Prophet

Yet, even after all the evidence and all the verses, most Sunnis and Shia will still claim that this is not all that the Messenger delivered, and that we should follow his example as contained in other texts or which we learn about through the holy Imams. Such people forget that the true example of the Prophet Mohammed, like the true example of the Prophet Abraham, has been recorded and captured in the Scripture for all time:

> *"Indeed, in the messenger of God a good example* (Uswa Hasana) *has been set for you for he who seeks God and the Last Day and thinks constantly about God." (Qur'an 33:21)*

> *"There has been a good example* (Uswa Hasana) *set for you by Abraham and those with him, when they said to their people: 'We are innocent from you and what you serve besides God. We have rejected you, and it appears that there shall be animosity and hatred between us and you until you believe in God alone.' Except for the saying of Abraham to his father: 'I will ask forgiveness for you, but I do not possess any power to protect you from God.' 'Our Lord, we have put our trust in You, and we turn to You, and to You is the final destiny.'" (Qur'an 60:4)*

The Messenger faced a terrifying challenge in delivering the word of God to a people who were accustomed to a way of life and traditions that completely contradicted the system of God. It was this Messenger that stood in the face of overwhelming odds, continued to have faith and patience and always knew that he must serve God Alone, even if all the people were telling him otherwise.

"Or did you expect that you would enter the Paradise, while the example of those who were before you came to you; they were stricken with adversity and hardship, and they were shaken until the messenger and those who believed with him said: 'When is the victory of God?' Yes indeed, the victory of God is near." (Qur'an 2:214)

The Scripture not only contains the laws of God, but it also contains beautiful examples of the life of the Prophet:

- His dealing with the idol worshippers. (53:19-23)

- His compassion towards the believers. (3:31)

- His love and constant remembrance of God. (33:21)

- His human fear of failing. (2:214)

- His dealing with his wives' rebellion. (33:28-31)

- His dealing with his adopted son. (33:37)

- His weakness in paying too much attention to the rich and powerful. (80:1-12)

All these and many more examples are contained within the precious book that God has honored. The life of the Messenger gives us frail humans *hope* that it is indeed possible to live the way God intended us to live (as described in the Scripture) and to uphold His covenant in spite of all adversity. Without the example of the Messenger, we may not even have bothered to read or study the Scripture for fear that it was an impractical book which required too much of human beings and described a fictional utopian society.

4

Back to Basics

Most Muslims, even after learning about the stark differences between today's distorted Sunni and Shia versions of Islam and the Islam of God and His Messenger, will have no problem living under any system of government (capitalist, communist, dictatorship, monarchy, or otherwise) as long as they are allowed to perform their rituals (whatever these rituals may be) in the belief that they are adhering to and following "the religion."

Is religion a collection of words and rituals that must be followed?

Or is it much more than that?

Let us turn to the Scripture for the answer...

> *[Yusuf Ali Translation 3:85]: If anyone desires a religion other than Islam (submission to Allah), never will it be accepted of him; and in the Hereafter He will be in the ranks of those who have lost (all spiritual good).*

This sounds pretty severe!

Does this mean that God is ordering us to follow some religion that goes by the name of Islam/Submission?

Are we to simply hunt down this Islam and apply its laws and rituals and let the matter rest there?

When we find this Islam, do we then force everyone else to follow and accept it?

> *[Yusuf Ali Translation 3:83]: Do they seek for other than the Religion of Allah?–while all creatures in the heavens and on earth have, willing or unwilling, bowed to His Will (accepted Islam), and to Him shall they all be brought back.*

If everything in the heavens has submitted to the religion of God, then who are we to argue?

> *[Yusuf Ali Translation 9:33]: It is He Who hath sent His Messenger with guidance and the Religion of Truth, to proclaim it over all religion, even though the Pagans may detest (it).*

A religion will dominate and expose other religions?

Does this mean that this Islam will, when we pray with our hands to our sides, "expose" those other religions whose adherents pray with their hands folded?

Or, does it mean that, when we give to charity, it will "expose" the other religions whose adherents also give to charity?

43

Obviously, none of this makes any sense!

> *[Pickthall Translation 9:36]: Lo! the number of the months with Allah is twelve months by Allah's ordinance in the day that He created the heavens and the earth. Four of them are sacred: that is the right religion. So wrong not yourselves in them. And wage war on all of the idolaters as they are waging war on all of you. And know that Allah is with those who keep their duty (unto Him).*

How are 12 months considered a correct religion?
What about using 19 months or 10 or 13?
Is that not still a religion?!

What is Religion?

Obviously, religion is not merely a collection of laws and rituals.

Let us look at the story of Joseph, which reveals the true meaning of religion. When we read the story of Joseph in chapter 12 of the Scripture, we learn that he went to Egypt and after a few incidents, became one of the high counselors of the king responsible for the distribution of food and commerce.

The brothers of Joseph (who had tried to kill him earlier) approached Joseph without recognizing him. Since he wanted to enlist his younger brother to join him without alerting his other brothers, he set up a scheme whereby the measuring bowl of the king was placed in the belongings of his younger brother.

The scheme was to let his brothers reveal the law of theft as it stood in their own religion. This law was used by Abraham and Jacob and revealed by God:

> *"They said: 'What shall be the punishment, if you are not truthful?' They (Joseph's brothers) said: 'The punishment is that he in whose saddlebag it is found*

will himself serve as the punishment. It is so that we punish the wicked."' (Qur'an 12:74-75)

After snaring his brothers in his trap and letting them expose the law that they followed (rather than using that of the king) Joseph was able to keep his younger brother with him:

> *[Yusuf Ali Translation 12:76]: So he began (the search) with their baggage, before (he came to) the baggage of his brother: at length he brought it out of his brother's baggage. Thus did We plan for Joseph. He could not take his brother by the law³ of the king except that Allah willed it (so). We raise to degrees (of wisdom) whom We please: but over all endowed with knowledge is one, the All-Knowing.*

Obviously, the king of Egypt did not have a religious law that he implemented for the crime of theft, but he did have a *system*.

Thus it was that Joseph bypassed the system of the king and replaced it with the one used by his brothers!

Religion = System

God clarifies the revelations that we may understand…

God has not given us a religion made up of strange components and rituals, but rather a perfect system that He has decreed through all His prophets:

> *"He has decreed for you the same (Deen) [system] He ordained for Noah, and what We inspired to you, and what We ordained for Abraham, Moses, and Jesus: 'You shall uphold this (Deen) [system], and do not divide in it.' Intolerable for the polytheists is what you invite them towards. God chooses for Himself*

---

3 The word 'law' as translated by Yusuf Ali is the Arabic word 'Deen' which has elsewhere been translated as 'religion.'

whoever He wills; He guides to Himself those who repent." (Qur'an 42:13)

God is our Maker. He did not construct the universe or our minds, bodies, and souls just so we could stumble and be lost in this world.

We have been given free will. We are free to choose whatever paths we desire. We are free to come up with as many systems we like.

However, He is bestowing great mercy on us by telling us that His system is the correct system:

"The count of the months with God is twelve months in the book of God the day He created the heavens and the earth; four of them are restricted. This is the correct system; so do not wrong yourselves in them; and fight the polytheists collectively as they fight you collectively. And know that God is with the righteous." (Qur'an 9:36)

There is nothing to stop us from using 11, 10 or even 19 months (that is what some of us do). However, although these systems may work, God is telling us that His is the best. We will not stumble when we properly use a 12-month count, which will keep us in line with the seasons and the movement of our planet.

All we need to do is just reach out our hands and grab hold of the rope that has been thrown down from heaven to us.

"Is it other than the system of God that they desire, when those in the heavens and the earth have submitted to Him voluntarily or by force? And to Him they will be returned." (Qur'an 3:83)

Do we see the sun having a problem with its orbit? Or, do we see the moon smashing into the Earth?

Each of these objects has taken up the system that was designed by God and followed it. Had they designed their own system, they would have been destroyed or knocked out of orbit eons ago.

Yet, we still falter!

We still think we know best!

We keep running different programs and systems, when, in the end, it is only one system that matches our nature.

> *"He is the One who has sent His messenger with the guidance and the system of truth, so that it will expose all other systems, even if the polytheists hate it." (Qur'an 9:33)*

It is only now that we understand what religion is that we can understand how it will *expose* all other religions.

The perfect system of God, when put into use, will reveal the weaknesses and shortcomings of all other systems invented by man...

The system of God is the only one that not only caters to the physical needs of the human being but also recognizes his spiritual needs and addresses those as well. The human that follows the system of God by submitting to it is not only a self-sufficient person but is also a happy person with strong family ties, intellectual capacity, philosophical views, community awareness and, above all, is a realist.

> *"...Today I have perfected your system for you, and completed My blessings upon you, and I have approved submission* (Islam) *as the system for you..." (Qur'an 5:3)*

5

Is This Islam?

While it may be difficult to accept that the Scripture has been abandoned by the masses, and that we have been following another religion altogether, this chapter will serve to highlight just some of the many differences that exist between today's Sunni and Shia Islam and the Islam decreed and authorized by God and His Messenger in the Scripture:

Inventing Pillars for Salvation

"Surely those who believe; and those who are Jewish,

and the Sabians, and the Nazarenes, whoever of them believes in God and the Last Day and does good works; then they will have nothing to fear nor will they grieve." (Qur'an 5:69)

As the centuries have gone by, Sunni and Shia scholars and Hadith followers have decided that the mercy of God as mentioned in 5:69 above 'encompasses too many' and thus they found the need to invent new rules for salvation by stating that Muslims can only be those who adhere to a set of pillars as defined by their scholars.

The Sunnis came up with a total of five main pillars, while the Shia decided that ten pillars was the way to go.

The 5-pillars of Sunnism:

1. Testifying there is no god but God and Mohammed is His messenger "Shahada."

2. Performing the five Obligatory Prayers "Salat."

3. Paying the annual 2.5 percent tax "Zakat."

4. Fasting during the month of Ramadhan "Sawm."

5. Making a pilgrimage to Mecca (once in a lifetime) if one is able "Hajj."

The 10-pillars of Shiaism:

1. Performing the Obligatory Prayers "Salat."

2. Fasting the month of Ramadhan "Sawm."

3. Pilgrimage "Hajj."

4. Paying a tax for the poor "Zakat."

5. Paying of the one-fifth of income to Ahlul Bayt "Khums."

6. Struggle "Jihad."

7. Enjoining what is good "Amr-Bil-Ma'ruf."

8. Forbidding what is evil "Nahi-Anil-Munkar."

9. To love Ahlul Bayt and their followers "Tawalla."

10. To disassociate from the enemies of Ahlul Bayt "Tabarra."

As shocking as it may sound, neither the "5 pillars" nor the "10 pillars" as they exist have been decreed in the Scripture as the way to salvation, and, as will be seen throughout this book, some of them are in clear violation of what has been stated by God and His Messenger.

Mentioning Others Besides God in His Own Temples

"And the temples are for God, so do not call on anyone alongside God." (Qur'an 72:18)

The Sunni and Shia are guilty of, amongst other things following the innovations that require them to praise, glorify, and call upon Mohammed and Abraham (by sending them salutations), thus nullifying the command of God not to call on anyone else besides Him in worship.

Is This How You Do Your Ablution (Wudu)?

"O you who believe, if you rise to hold the contact prayer (Salat), then wash your faces and your hands up to the elbows, and wipe your heads and your feet to the ankles; and if you have had intercourse, then you shall bathe. And if you are ill, or traveling, or you have excreted feces, or you have had sexual contact with the women, and you cannot not find water, then you shall select from the clean soil; you shall wipe your faces and your hands with it. God does not want to place any hardship on you, but He wants to cleanse you and to complete His blessings upon you that you may be thankful." (Qur'an 5:6)

While the preparation for the Salat is straightforward and simple, the masses have turned such a simple command into an entire ritual that includes special words to be said, the wiping of the ears and blowing of nostrils etc.

Circumcising Males

> "God is the One who made the earth a habitat for you, and the heaven as a structure, and He designed you, and has perfected your design. And He provided you with good provisions. Such is God your Lord. Most Exalted is God, Lord of the worlds." (Qur'an 40:64)

God speaks of His creation as having been "perfected," and, while the masses openly agree with this statement, they act against it by trying to complete the work of God by cutting off some of the male foreskin (in some cases, even females have been circumcised, but that is for a different reason i.e. a barbaric attempt to suppress the natural female sexual drive!).

In fact, it was one of the promises of the devil himself that he would influence humankind so that they would make alterations to the perfect creation of God:

> "'And I will misguide them and make them desire, and I will command them, so that they will mark the ears of the livestock, and I will command them so they will make changes to the creation of God.' Whoever takes the devil as a supporter other than God, then he has indeed lost a great loss." (Qur'an 4:119)

The origin of circumcision can be traced back to the Jewish Bible:

> [Gen 17:14.13] Any uncircumcised male who is not circumcised in the flesh of his foreskin shall be cut off from his people; he has broken my covenant.

[Gen 17:24.16] Abraham was ninety-nine years old when he was circumcised in the flesh of his foreskin.

The sects seem to have been misled into following the questionable acts of the modern Jewish Bible while they have been clearly commanded to adhere to the Qur'an that overrides and supersedes any previous scriptures!

Lawful and Forbidden (Halal And Haram)

"Forbidden to you is that which is already dead, and the blood, and the meat of pig, and what was dedicated to other than God, and that which has been strangled, and that which has been beaten to death, and that which has fallen from a height, and that which has been gored, and that which the wild animals have eaten from except what you managed to rescue, and what has been slaughtered on altars, and what you divide by the arrows of chance. This is wickedness. Today the rejecters have given up from your system, so do not be concerned by them, but be concerned by Me. Today I have perfected your system for you, and completed My blessings upon you, and I have approved submission as the system for you. So, whoever is forced by severe hunger and not seeking sin, then God is Forgiving, Merciful." (Qur'an 5:3)

"Say: 'Have you seen what God has sent down to you from provisions, then you have made some of it unlawful and some lawful?' Say: 'Did God authorize you, or do you invent lies about God?' And what will those who invent lies about God think on the Day of Resurrection? God is with great bounty to the people, but most of them are not thankful." (Qur'an 10:59-60)

Of course, these clear instructions were not clear enough for the sects who went on to forbid carnivorous animals, pig product derivatives (which are not made from the meat), alcohol and its by-products etc.

Breaking the Fast at Sunset/Dusk

"It has been made lawful for you during the night of fasting to approach your women sexually. They are a garment for you and you are a garment for them. God knows that you used to betray your souls so He has accepted your repentance, and forgiven you; now you may approach them and seek what God has written for you. And you may eat and drink until the white thread is distinct from the black thread of dawn; then you shall complete the fast until night; and do not approach them while you are devoted in the temples. These are the boundaries of God, so do not transgress them. It is thus that God clarifies His revelations to the people who they may be righteous." (Qur'an 2:187)

God tells us that we are to fast until night has come. Yet, the Sunni masses insist on blatantly disobeying His command by breaking the fast while there is still light, i.e. at sunset, based on the innovation of the Hadiths, clearly ignoring the definition of night as the absence of light (36:37), or that dawn, like dusk, is defined as a part of the day (11:114).

Propagating "Intercession" on Judgment Day

"O you who believe, spend from what We have provided for you before a Day comes when there is no trade, nor friendship, nor intercession; and the disbelievers are the wicked." (Qur'an 2:254)

"And beware of a Day when no soul can avail another soul, nor will any amendment be accepted from it, nor will any intercession help it; they will not be supported." (Qur'an 2:123)

Although the Qur'an repeatedly states that there will be no human intercession on the Day of Judgment, the masses have insisted on idolizing the Prophet against his will, and believing in the invented concept of intercession (Shafaa'ah).

God only allows human 'intercession' that is done for the good of people and that takes place on Earth while we are still alive.

"Whoever intercedes with a good intercession, he will have a reward of it; and whoever intercedes with an evil intercession, he will receive a share of it. And God has control over all things." (Qur'an 4:85)

"Say: 'To God belongs all intercession.' To Him belongs the sovereignty of the heavens and the earth, then to Him you will be returned. And when God Alone is mentioned, the hearts of those who do not believe in the Hereafter are filled with aversion; and when others are mentioned besides Him, they rejoice!" (Qur'an 39:44-45)

When an intercession is made, it is up to God to accept or reject it based on His judgment and based on the condition/standing of the person making the request and the condition/standing of the person on whose behalf the intercession is made.

Claiming Prophet Mohammed Predicted the Future

"Say: 'I do not say to you that I possess the treasures of God, nor do I know the future, nor do I say to you that I am an angel. I merely follow what is inspired

> *to me.' Say: 'Are the blind and the seer the same? Do you not think?'" (Qur'an 6:50)*

In the clearest words, the Prophet Mohammed declares that he does not know the future. Yet, we have hundreds of tales being spun by Sunnis and Shias regarding future events and predictions ranging from the four *Khalifas* who will rule after his death, and an immortal one-eyed man named Al-Dajjal who is supposed to possess superhuman powers and who will ravage the Earth, to Jesus coming back!

Exalting Some Prophets Over Others

> *"Say: 'We believe in God and in what was sent down to us and what was sent down to Abraham, and Ishmael, and Isaac, and Jacob, and the Patriarchs, and what was given to Moses and Jesus, and what was given to the prophets from their Lord; we do not make a distinction between any of them and to Him we submit.'" (Qur'an 2:136)*

> *"The messenger believes in what was sent down to him from his Lord. And the believers, all who believe in God, and His angels, and His Books, and His messengers: 'We do not make a distinction between any of His messengers;' and they said: 'We hear and obey, forgive us O Lord, and to you is our destiny.'" (Qur'an 2:285)*

Muslims are required to treat all of the messengers of God as being equal and not to differentiate between any of them. However, we have countless cases of today's Sunnis and Shia exalting the Prophet Mohammed (and his family) above all other prophets and messengers by stating he was the 'most honorable' messenger, mentioning his name in their daily Salat, invoking an honorific title "Salalahu Aliyhi Wa Salam" at every mention of his name, stating that the Prophet performed miracles not mentioned in the authentic history captured in the Scripture, stating that the Prophet has powers of intercession to save the sinners from amongst his followers, etc.

Stoning Adulterers to Death

> *"The adulteress and the adulterer, you shall lash each of them with one hundred lashes, and do not let any pity overtake you regarding the system of God if you believe in God and the Last Day. And let a group of the believers witness their punishment." (Qur'an 24:2)*

The law which applies in the case of proven adultery involving independent females (Muhsanat) is to punish the adulterers with one hundred lashes.

Do the Sunnis and Shia follow and obey this law?

The Sunni and Shia scholars declared that the law in the Scripture is not clear. They claimed that the adulterers are not defined in the Scripture as far as their marital status is concerned, and thus they instituted 'stoning to death' as the punishment for married adulterers.

More investigation reveals that the masses are once again following the teachings passed down through the Jewish rabbis and biblical scriptures where the punishment for adultery is stoning to death.

> [Deut 22:20—21] But if the thing is true, that the tokens of virginity were not found in the young woman, then they shall bring out the young woman to the door of her father's house, and the men of her city shall stone her to death with stones, because she has wrought folly in Israel by playing the harlot in her father's house; so you shall purge the evil from the midst of you.
>
> [Lev 20:10] If a man commits adultery with the wife of his neighbor, both the adulterer and the

adulteress shall be put to death.

Will the masses plead ignorance on Judgment Day for blatantly following questionable laws other than those found in the Qur'an?

Cutting the Hands of Thieves

> *[Yusuf Ali Translation 5:38]: As to the thief, Male or female, cut off his or her hands: a punishment by way of example, from Allah, for their crime: and Allah is Exalted in power.*

The subject of theft has been one that causes much controversy in its traditional understanding and application throughout the Muslim world. The scholars of today and the past have all subscribed to the punishment of cutting off of the hands and thus we witness scenes of amputations being carried out in countries that claim to uphold the Qur'an. However, had they carried out the extra step of looking at the "examples" within the Qur'an for guidance, they would have come to a far different conclusion.

The story of Joseph and his brothers provides the clearest and simplest example for how to deal with the subject of theft…

> "*They said: 'By God, you know we have not come to cause corruption in the land, and we are not thieves!' They said: 'What shall be the punishment, if you are not truthful?' They said: 'The punishment is that he in whose saddlebag it is found will himself serve as the punishment. It is so that we punish the wicked.'*" (Qur'an 12:73-75)

The law of God that Joseph applied against his brother in the matter of theft did not lead to any amputation of the hand or any other mindless act of violence. It did, however, lead to the brother being made to remain behind and work as against the value of the item which he was accused of stealing.

Looking back at verse 5:38, and if we apply the correct translation, we get a completely different understanding from that of Yusuf Ali:

> *"As for the thief, both male and female, you shall cut from their resources – as a penalty for what they have earned – to be made an example of from God. God is Noble, Wise." (Qur'an 5:38)*

The correct understanding of the verse not only matches the example of the punishment for theft given in the Scripture, but it is also in line with the other checks and balances that God has laid down, such as the requirement that the punishment should not exceed the crime (16:126).

Prohibiting Women from Salat During Menstruation

> *"O you who believe, if you rise to hold the contact prayer (Salat), then wash your faces and your hands up to the elbows, and wipe your heads and your feet to the ankles; and if you have had intercourse, then you shall bathe. And if you are ill, or traveling, or you have excreted feces, or you have had sexual contact with the women, and you cannot not find water, then you shall select from the clean soil; you shall wipe your faces and your hands with it. God does not want to place any hardship on you, but He wants to cleanse you and to complete His blessings upon you that you may be thankful." (Qur'an 5:6)*

While God has clearly outlined for His people what causes the ablution to become nullified, the Sunni and Shia scholars have invented their own list to rival that of God. This list includes menstruating women, eating camel meat, and touching dogs.

Prohibiting Men from Wearing Gold and Silk

> "Say: 'Who has made unlawful the nice things that God has brought forth for His servants and the good provisions?' Say: 'They are meant for those who believe during this worldly life, and they will be exclusive for them on the Day of Resurrection.' It is such that We explain the revelations for those who know." (Qur'an 7:32)

To prohibit what God has made lawful is severe to say the least. Prohibiting men from wearing gold and silk is one of the many innovations the scholars have concocted.

Prohibiting Art and Music

> "They made for him what he desired of enclosures, and images and pools of deep reservoirs, and heavy pots. 'O family of David, work to give thanks.' Only a few of My servants are thankful." (Qur'an 34:13)

Not only are the arts and music *not* forbidden in the Qur'an (which makes them automatically permissible), but we also have an example of Solomon commissioning the making of statues and verses stating that beautiful and humble voices are encouraged. All this is a far cry from the prohibitions that have been falsely attributed to God and His messenger.

Prohibiting the Keeping of Dogs for Domestic Use

> "And you would think they are awake while they are asleep. And We turn them on the right-side and on the left-side, and their dog has his arms outstretched at the threshold. If you looked upon them you would have run away from them and you would have been filled with terror from them!" (Qur'an 18:18)

Humankind has been using dogs for hunting and for domestic purposes (as pets) for as long as history has been recorded. The Qur'an even honored the dog in the famous story of the sleepers of the cave, "Ahlul Kahf," by mentioning that a dog was among those who were asleep for around 300 years. Yet, in one move, the Sunnis and Shia who continue to disregard the Qur'an declared that dogs were unclean and that they cannot be kept for domestic use but may only be used for hunting or protection. They invented ridiculous stories about the devil appearing in the form of a black dog and they insist that if a person touches a dog, then he/she must wash seven times before being able to pray. As a result, millions upon millions of Muslim children have been denied the pleasure of having a dog as a pet.

Advocating the Killing of Apostates

> *"There is no compulsion in the system; the proper way has been clarified from the wrong way. Whoever rejects evil, and believes in God, indeed he has taken grasp of the strongest hold that will never break. God is Hearer, Knower." (Qur'an 2:256)*

The Qur'an states frequently that there is no compulsion in religion (2:256; 10:99; 88:21-22).

The Qur'an advocates freedom of belief and expression (18:29).

However, the Sunnis and Shia have converted this system of knowledge and reason into a mafia organization, where, once you enter, you can never leave!

> [Bukhari, Volume 9, Book 83, Number 17: Narrated Abdullah] Allah's Messenger said, "The blood of a Muslim who confesses that none has the right to be worshipped but Allah and that I am His Messenger, cannot be shed except in

three cases: in Qisas (equality in punishment) for murder, a married person who commits illegal sexual intercourse and the one who reverts from Islam (Apostate) and leaves the Muslims."

Allowing a Man to Marry Up to Four Wives

"And give the orphans their money, and do not replace the good with the bad, and do not consume their money with your money; for truly this is a great sin! And if you fear that you cannot be just to the orphans, then you may marry those who are agreeable to you of the women: two, and three, and four. But if you fear you will not be fair, then only one, or whom you maintain by your oaths. This is best that you do not face financial hardship." (Qur'an 4:2-3)

Today's Sunnis and Shia believe that due to their high sexual libido, God has given them an "open license" to marry up to four women to satisfy some ancient *homo sapien* sexual need.

What these traditionalists have conveniently overlooked is that marriage to more than one wife is *restricted* to the presence of orphans and thus the women mentioned are in fact the mothers of orphans already under the guardianship of a man.

The license for polygamy is not a license to indulge one's sexual desire and fantasies, but is driven by a concern for the welfare of orphans and human compassion so as to incorporate the orphaned family as permanent members and equals into the household they are already living in.

Nullifying the Divorce Laws of the Scripture

> *"O you prophet, if any of you have divorced the women, then they should be divorced while ensuring that their required interim is fulfilled, and keep count of the interim. You shall reverence God your Lord, and do not evict them from their homes, nor should they leave, unless they commit an evident lewdness. And these are the boundaries of God. And anyone who transgresses the boundaries of God has wronged his soul. You never know; perhaps God will make something come out of this." (Qur'an 65:1)*

The Qur'an is very strict on the subject of divorce and highlights the need for a three-month interim period. The interim period is critical in that the couple must remain under the same roof. At any time during this phase, the divorce proceedings may be cancelled and the marriage resumed.

Compare this to the destructive divorce laws practiced by today's scholars whereby the man can divorce the mother of his children on the spot by simply uttering the words "you are divorced" and where the 'interim' period requiring them to remain together is completely ignored!

Denying Wills and Testaments

> *"God directs you regarding the inheritance of your children: 'To the male shall be as that given to two females. If they are women, more than two, then they will have two thirds of what is inherited. And if she is only one, then she will have one half. And to his parents, each one of them shall have one sixth of what is inherited, if he has a child. If he has no child and his parents are the heirs, then to his mother is one third; if he has siblings then to his mother is one sixth. All after a will is carried through or a debt. Your parents and your children, you do not know which are closer*

to you in benefit, a directive from God, for God is Knowledgeable, Wise.'" (Qur'an 4:11)

The Qur'an only allows its inheritance guidelines to be used if there is no will and testament, or if there is inheritance still left over after the stipulations of a will and testament have been carried out. As can be expected, the scholars have decided to oppose the law of God and have stated that a will and testament becomes null and void if the deceased has descendants.

Testifying to the Messengership of the Prophet

"When the hypocrites come to you they say: 'We bear witness that you are the messenger of God.' And God knows that you are His messenger, and God bears witness that the hypocrites are liars." (Qur'an 63:1)

"Any good that befalls you is from God, and any evil that befalls you is from yourself. We have sent you as a messenger to the people and God is enough as a witness." (Qur'an 4:79)

Although God says that He is *enough* as a witness to the messengership of the Prophet, the masses insist on not believing the words of the Lord by giving testimony (saying: "we bear witness that Mohammed is the messenger of God") to this effect each and every day.

They have thus fallen into the same trap that those during the time of the Prophet had fallen into... of saying with their mouths the words that prove that their hearts deny the truth.

What Have We Done!

The above examples are merely the tip of the iceberg and the contradictions between the Sunni and Shia versions of Islam and the Islam taught to us by God and His Messenger run much wider and deeper, ranging from the structure of government, to the count of the year, to the taxation imposed, etc. It is therefore no wonder that the wrath of God is upon us and that we are destined for humiliation and destruction unless we mend our ways and change.

All we had to do was verify what we were being constantly told and taught and none of this mess would have happened…

> *"And do not uphold what you have no knowledge of. For the hearing, eyesight, and mind, all these you are responsible for." (Qur'an 17:36)*

God has called us neither Sunni nor Shia nor has He advocated the laws that the masses currently impose in His name, but He has called us Muslims (those who have submitted) since the days of our father Abraham, and that is a name we should all proudly carry.

> *"And strive in the cause of God its truly deserved striving. He is the One who has chosen you, and He has made no hardship for you in the system, the creed of your father Abraham; He is the One who named you 'those who have submitted' from before and in this. So let the messenger be witness over you and you be witness over the people. So hold the contact prayer and contribute towards purification and hold tight to God, He is your patron. What an excellent Patron, and what an excellent Supporter." (Qur'an 22:78)*

May God forgive us for all the wrong that we have done…

6

Social Responsibility

Besides the laws revealed by God that were designed to govern our lives, and which are covered in later chapters, the Scripture has also listed some rules of etiquette, which we are advised to apply in our dealings with each other.

> *"This Qur'an guides to that which is more upright, and it gives glad tidings to the believers who do good works that they will have a bountiful reward." (Qur'an 17:9)*

The following list does not contain laws (in the legal sense), but when God makes a recommendation, it is always advisable for us to "hear and obey" for this will guarantee happiness for all involved.

Always Respond to a Greeting

"And if you are greeted with a greeting, then return an even better greeting or return the same. God is Reckoning over all things." (Qur'an 4:86)

Say Good Things

"Have you not seen how God puts forth the example that a good word is like a good tree, whose root is firm and whose branches are in the heaven. It bears its fruit every so often with the permission of its Lord; and God puts forth the examples for the people, perhaps they will remember." (Qur'an 14:24–25)

Be Humble and Speak Lightly

"'And be humble in how you walk and lower your voice. For the harshest of all voices is the voice of the donkeys.'" (Qur'an 31:19)

Invite to God with Wisdom and Kindness

"Invite to the path of your Lord with wisdom and good advice, and argue with them in that which is better. Your Lord is fully aware of who is misguided from His path, and He is fully aware of the guided ones." (Qur'an 16:125)

"It was a mercy from God that you were soft towards them; had you been harsh and mean hearted, they would have dispersed from you; so pardon them and ask

forgiveness for them, and consult them in the matter; but when you are convinced, then put your trust in God; for God loves those who put their trust." (Qur'an 3:159)

Be Kind to Your Parents

"And your Lord decreed that you shall not serve except He, and do good to your parents. When one of them or both of them reach old age, do not say to them a word of disrespect nor shout at them, but say to them a kind saying. And lower for them the wing of humility through mercy, and say: 'My Lord, have mercy upon them as they have raised me when I was small.'" (Qur'an 17:23-24)

Suppress Anger and Forgive People

"And race towards forgiveness from your Lord and a Paradise whose width encompasses the width of the heavens and of the earth; it has been prepared for the righteous. The ones who spend in prosperity and adversity, and who repress anger, and who pardon the people; God loves the good doers." (Qur'an 3:133-134)

Counter Evil with Good

"Not equal are the good and the bad response. You shall resort to the one which is better. Thus, the one who used to be your enemy, may become your best friend." (Qur'an 41:34)

"And those who are patient seeking the face of their Lord; and they hold the contact prayer, and they spend from what We have bestowed upon them secretly and

openly, and they counter evil with good; these will have an excellent abode." (Qur'an 13:22)

Do Not Say Bad Things

"And the example of a bad word is like a tree which has been uprooted from the surface of the earth, it has nowhere to settle." (Qur'an 14:26)

Do Not Be Arrogant or Carefree

"'And do not turn your cheek arrogantly from people, nor shall you roam the earth insolently. For God does not love the arrogant show off.'" (Qur'an 31:18)

Do Not Engage in Ignorant Talk

"And the servants of the Almighty who walk on the earth in humility and if the ignorant speak to them, they say: 'Peace.'" (Qur'an 25:63)

Do Not Insult the Idolaters

"And do not insult those who call on other than God, lest they insult God out of ignorance. And We have similarly adorned for every nation their works; then to their Lord is their return and He will inform them of what they had done." (Qur'an 6:108)

Do Not Make Fun of Others or Call Them Names

"O you who believe, let not a people ridicule other people, for they may be better than they. Nor shall any women ridicule other women, for they may be better than they. Nor shall you mock one another, or call each

*other names; miserable indeed is the name of wicked-
ness after attaining faith. And anyone who does not repent, then these are the transgressors." (Qur'an 49:11)*

Do Not Be Suspicious, Spy, or Backbite

*"O you who believe, if a wicked person comes to you
with any news, then you shall investigate it. Lest you
harm a people out of ignorance, then you will become
regretful over what you have done." (Qur'an 49:6)*

*"O you who believe, you shall avoid much suspicion,
for some suspicion is sinful. And do not spy on one
another, nor shall you backbite. Would any of you
enjoy eating the flesh of his dead brother? You
certainly would hate this. You shall observe God. God
is Redeemer, Merciful." (Qur'an 49:12)*

Do Not Be Racist

*"O mankind, We created you from a male and female,
and We made you into nations and tribes, that you
may know one another. Surely, the most honorable
among you in the sight of God is the most righteous.
God is Knowledgeable, Expert." (Qur'an 49:13)*

Jihad/Striving

The word "Jihad" has been used by the media and even
the Muslim masses as a synonym for "Holy War." Thus,
supposedly, when Muslims are about to go to war or fight
an enemy, they declare "Jihad" against that enemy and all
the faithful are expected to march bravely and mobilize
against such an enemy.

What we find is that the word "Jihad" is used in the
Scripture in relation to the general act of struggling or

striving and has never been used, as falsely claimed, solely as a declaration of some fanatical holy war to be waged against the infidels and their allies.

Below are verses that use the word "Jihad" and whose meaning is self-evident:

"And We instructed the human being to be good to his parents. But if they strive (Jahada) *to make you set up partners with Me, then do not obey them. To Me are all your destinies, and I will inform you of what you used to do." (Qur'an 29:8)*

"If they strive (Jahadaka) *to make you set up any partners besides Me, then do not obey them. But continue to treat them amicably in this world. You shall follow only the path of those who have sought Me. Ultimately, you all return to Me, then I will inform you of everything you have done." (Qur'an 31:15)*

"Those who believe, and those who have immigrated and strived (Jahadu) *in the cause of God; these are seeking the mercy of God; and God is Forgiving, Merciful." (Qur'an 2:218)*

"Or did you think that you would enter the Paradise without God distinguishing those who would strive (Jahadu) *among you and distinguishing those who are patient?" (Qur'an 3:142)*

"Those who have believed and emigrated and strived (Jahadu) *with their money and lives in the cause of God, and those who have sheltered and supported; these are the allies of one another. And those who believed but did not emigrate, you do not owe them any obligation until they emigrate. But if they seek*

*your help in the system, then you must support them,
except if it is against a people with whom there is a
covenant between you and them. And God is Seer over
what you do." (Qur'an 8:72)*

*"Those who have remained are happy with their
position of lagging behind the messenger of God, and
they disliked striving (Yujahidu) with their money
and lives in the cause of God; and they say: 'Do not
mobilize in the heat.' Say: 'The fire of Hell is much
hotter,' if they could only understand." (Qur'an 9:81)*

Slaves and Concubines

The Qur'an had come as a light and beacon for humankind
so that it could regulate social relations and to guide the
believing men and women. However, we see a strange
pattern of behavior among the Sunni and Shia masses
whereby they have legitimized the owning of slaves and
concubines for nothing more than sexual pleasure and
satisfaction!

Of course, to commit a sin and then claim that God
allowed it is not new to humankind:

*"And if they commit evil acts, they say: 'We found our
fathers doing such, and God ordered us to it.' Say: 'God
does not order evil! Do you say about God what you do
not know?'" (Qur'an 7:28)*

The truth of the matter is that the Qur'an does not,
under any circumstances, allow for slaves or concubines.

What Is the "License" Regarding Servants?

*"And marry off those among you that are single, and
the good from among your male and female servants
(Ibadikum). If they are poor, then God will grant*

71

them from His grace. And God is Encompassing, Knowledgeable." (Qur'an 24:32)

Clearly, the Qur'an gives no license for a person to have illicit sexual relations with his/her servant but rather speaks of helping them get married as an act of righteousness.

What about Slaves?

The Qur'an requires in many repeated verses that slaves be set free as an act of true righteousness. At the same time, there are no verses allowing the creation of new slaves. Thus, if no one is being enslaved while existing slaves are being set free, then the issue of slavery becomes a non-issue within a short period of time for any nation/state being governed by the Qur'an.

> *"Piety is not to turn your faces towards the east and the west, but pious is one who believes in God and the Last Day, and the angels, and the Book, and the prophets, and who gives money out of love to the relatives, and the orphans, and the needy, and the wayfarer, and those who ask, and to free the slaves; and who upholds the contact prayer, and who contributes towards purification; and those who keep their pledges when they make a pledge, and those who are patient in the face of hardship and adversity and when in despair. These are the ones who have been truthful, and these are the righteous." (Qur'an 2:177)*

What about Captives?

The word in the Scripture for captives is "Asra." As expected, though the Qur'an speaks of captives and how they should be treated; it never, under any circumstances, provides a license for anyone to have sex with them or abuse them or rape them!

> *"And they give food out of love to the poor and the orphan and the captive. 'We only feed you seeking the face of God; we do not desire from you any reward or thanks.'"* (Qur'an 76:8-9)

What about "Ma Malakat Aymanukum"?

The last sectarian jab at trying to find ways of having illicit sex comes under the deliberate misinterpretation of "Ma Malakat Aymanukum." It is argued that the Qur'an gives license to have sex with this category of women, which means that concubines are permitted.

The people who put forward such arguments apparently do not care to read the Qur'an closely, else they would have spotted the following verse:

> *"And whoever of you cannot afford to marry the independent female believers, then from those maintained by your oaths* (Ma Malakat Aymanukum) *of the believing young women. And God is more aware of your faith, some of you to each other. You shall marry them with the permission of their parents and give them their dowries in kindness; to be independent, not for illicit sex or taking lovers. When they become independent, then any of them who come with lewdness shall have half of what is the punishment for those independent. This is for those who are concerned about deviating from among you. But if you are patient it is better for you, and God is Forgiver, Merciful."* (Qur'an 4:25)

In the clearest of possible words, God is telling us that the people from this category (which includes males as well as females 24:31) are young people who are still under guardianship, and who can only be entered into a relationship with under *marriage*, and that such marriage requires the approval of their parents/guardians.

So much for concubines!

The Independent Women (Muhsanat)

To finish the discussion regarding the categories of women and the requirement for their marriage, it is worth looking at the verses that deal with women who have become "independent":

> *"And the independent from the women, except those maintained by your oaths; the book of God over you; and permitted for you is what is beyond this, if you are seeking with your money to be independent, not for illicit sex. As for those whom you have already had joy with, then you shall give them their dowries as an obligation. There is no sin upon you for what you agree on after the obligation. God is Knowledgeable, Wise. And whoever of you cannot afford to marry the independent female believers, then from those maintained by your oaths of the believing young women. And God is more aware of your faith, some of you to each other. You shall marry them with the permission of their parents and give them their dowries in kindness; to be independent, not for illicit sex or taking lovers. When they become independent, then any of them who come with lewdness shall have half of what is the punishment for those independent. This is for those who are concerned about deviating from among you. But if you are patient it is better for you, and God is Forgiver, Merciful." (Qur'an 4:24-25)*

A woman becomes "independent" (Muhsana) from her family/guardian by virtue of marriage (4:25) or, by self invocation of independence (24:33). Once a woman becomes "independent," then she retains such status for life, even if she becomes divorced or widowed. More importantly, the Qur'an encourages that "independent/

mature" women become the first choice for marriage over seeking younger partners (4:25).

Dress Code for Women

The Muslim nations of today take pride in the fact that most of their womenfolk wear headcovers when going out or at work. These women are considered sacred because they are adhering to the way of the Prophet and are thus representing the monotheistic faith. Few things identify an Islamic woman as quickly as the scarf the wearing of which is promoted in schools, through the media, and even in foreign countries where it has become a matter of identity, such as in France.

What if we dared say that the famous Islamic headscarf, called a Hijaab, has no basis in the Book of God and is therefore an innovation?

How would all those millions of devoted women and their men-folk feel knowing that they have been celebrating an achievement that has no basis in Islam and can rather be traced back to Rabbinical Judaism?

The Word "Hijab" In the Scripture?

The name of the headcover in today's Islam is Hijab. This word and its derivatives occur seven times in the Scripture, and not once do they refer to a headcover or are even related to dress as the masses have been led to believe. Here are the occurrences of the word "Hijab" in the Qur'an: 7:46, 17:46, 19:17, 33:53, 38:32, 41:5, and 42:51.

Four Dress Code Rules

The following four rules are what the Qur'an has to say about the dress code for women:

1. Righteousness is the Best Garment

"O Children of Adam, We have sent down for you gar-

ments to alleviate your sin, and feathers; and the garment of righteousness is the best. That is from the signs
of God, perhaps they will remember." (Qur'an 7:26)

2. Cover Your Private Parts

"And tell the believing females to lower their gaze and
keep covered their private parts..." (Qur'an 24:31)

3. Cover Your Breasts

"And tell the believing females to lower their gaze and
keep covered their private parts, and that they should
not reveal their beauty except what is apparent, and let
them put forth their shawls over their cleavage. And let
them not reveal their beauty except to their husbands,
or their fathers, or fathers of their husbands, or their
sons, or the sons of their husbands, or their brothers, or
the sons of their brothers, or the sons of their sisters, or
their women, or those maintained by their oaths, or the
male servants who are without need, or the child who
has not yet understood the composition of women. And
let them not strike with their feet in a manner that
reveals what they are keeping hidden of their beauty.
And repent to God, all of you believers, that you may
succeed." (Qur'an 24:31)

4. Dress Sensibly According to Situation

"O prophet, tell your wives, your daughters, and the
women of the believers that they should lengthen
upon themselves their outer garments. That is better
so that they will not be recognized and harmed. God
is Forgiver, Merciful." (Qur'an 33:59)

The issue of dress code takes on an entirely new dimension
if we revert back to the Scripture and stop following the

innovations that are designed to undermine the perfect system of God. Muslim women are to dress according to the situation/place they are in. If they are at the beach, then they may exercise the minimum dress code requirement by covering their genitalia and bosoms. If they are in a city setting, then the minimum becomes unacceptable as it will attract harm in most cases, and thus the woman is to dress conservatively (by lengthening her garments). This is the dynamic system of the Scripture, one that provides for the needs of the world as well as the requirements for the Hereafter.

What about the Order to Stay at Home in 33:33?

"You shall settle down in your homes, and do not go about like in the old days of ignorance. You shall hold the contact prayer, and contribute towards purification, and obey God and His messenger. God wishes to remove any affliction from you, O people of the Sanctuary, and to purify you completely." (Qur'an 33:33)

The wives of the Prophet are treated unlike other women (33:32) and thus have been given special rules and status in the Scripture that do not apply to the other believers. Here are some examples of the differences:

- If any of them commits lewdness, she receives double the punishment of ordinary believers. (33:30)

- If she does good works, then she is granted double the reward. (33:31)

- If the Prophet dies, then none of his wives may re-marry. (33:53)

As such, the laws that apply to the wives of the Prophet cannot be (and should not be) enforced on other believing women.

7

Economic System

The Scripture highlights the principle of economic development for humankind and establishes the guidelines and rules with which such principle is to operate.

> *"Wealth and sons are a beauty of this worldly life. But the good deeds that remain behind are better with your Lord for a reward, and better for hope." (Qur'an 18:46)*

The Value of Money

> "O you who believe, many of the Priests and Monks consume the money of the people in falsehood, and they repel from the path of God. And those who hoard gold and silver, and do not spend it in the cause of God, give them news of a painful retribution." (Qur'an 9:34)

Money is recognized as that which is coined from gold and/or silver or that which is printed and backed by gold and/or silver as an acceptable medium for exchange between people and/or entities.

Throughout history, gold and silver have been among the things most in demand due to their intrinsic industrial value and high processing and extraction costs.

The notion of using paper as money can be traced back to the late 1700s when the United States printed paper dollars called the continentals. A problem arose where people refused to exchange goods and services for mere paper. Hence, the U.S. saying "not worth a continental."

During the Civil War, the U.S. printed "greenback" paper money, which, as a currency, people similarly rejected. People recognized that the paper had no value, and thus, they would be trading their goods and services for virtually nothing. They simply were "not worth a greenback."

Convincing people to accept paper as currency or money was very cleverly achieved through a two-step approach:

1. Paper was issued and backed by a deposit of gold and silver held by the government. Thus, people were comfortable trading the paper, which, in reality, was a title to real gold or silver and which

had the following words written on it: "pay to the bearer on demand the value of…"

US Dollars Note—Backed by Gold and Silver

2. Once people became comfortable in exchanging goods and services using this paper, the governments of the world in succession removed the gold and silver backing from the paper by removing the statement "pay to the bearer" and thus all money thereafter became known as fiat money.

US Dollars Today—Backed by Nothing

Most people today are unaware of the injustice that has been committed, and that they are working hard for many years while being paid in paper. While some may argue that paper does have value because it is accepted by others as payment for goods and services, this myth is quickly exposed as soon as a government collapses or a state of war is declared. People who owned millions of fiat notes can no longer afford to even buy a meal as no trader is willing to accept what has apparently become just a piece of paper!

Using the Islamic principle of money coined or backed by gold and silver, we can see how even in the event of government collapse or war, the gold and silver will still retain its intrinsic value, and the purchasing power will only be affected by the laws of supply and demand. Thus, the foundation of money being based on gold and silver is in fact a foundation of justice.

Interest

"O you who believe, do not consume usury, compounding over and over; and reverence God that you may succeed." (Qur'an 3:130)

To examine the subject of "interest," we need to first define the word. Islamic scholars have conflicting opinions regarding the subject of interest. Is it any growth in money, even one percent? Or, is it an excessive growth in money, say more than 10 percent?

There are many books on the subject written by Islamic scholars with views against any growth, and views against excessive growth. One of the scholars at Al-Azhar University, Cairo, wrote a book on the subject some years back, and he came to the conclusion that the interest mentioned in the Scripture (called "Riba" in Arabic) was excessive interest. He had based these findings on a study of economic principles and the movement of goods and services, with the premise of his argument being: "If money doesn't grow, then there is no incentive to lend, which means stagnation in economic development."

To simplify our quest, we turn to the Scripture to understand the meaning of interest (Riba).

"And from among His signs is that you see the land still, then, as soon as We send down the water upon it, it shakes and grows (Rabat). Surely, the One who

revived it can revive the dead. He is capable of all things." (Qur'an 41:39)

Here, we read that the land, once it is fed by water, will grow (Rabat). This growth is given no measure, nor quantity, nor percentage.

Thus, in the simplest terms, we find that interest (Riba) is any growth. This understanding is confirmed in verse 30:39 below, which speaks of interest as being a 'growth' in the money of the people:

"And any usury you have taken to grow from the money of the people, it will not grow with God. And any contribution that you have placed seeking the face of God, then those will be multiplied." (Qur'an 30:39)

What Is the Ruling of the Scripture on Interest?

"Those who consume usury do not rise except as one being influenced by the touch of the devil. That is because they have said: "Trade is the same as usury." While God has made trade lawful, and He has made usury unlawful. Whoever has received understanding from His Lord and ceases, then he will be forgiven for what was before this and his case will be with God. But whoever returns, then they are the people of the Fire, in it they will abide. God condemns usury, and He grants growth to the charities. And God does not love any wicked sinner. Those who believe and do good works, and hold the contact prayer, and contribute towards purification; they will have their recompense with their Lord and there is no fear over them nor will they grieve. O you who believe, be aware of God and give up what is left from usury, if you are truly believers. And if you will not do this, then be aware of a war from God and His messenger; but if you repent, then

you will have back your principal money, you will not be wronged nor will you wrong." (Qur'an 2:275-279)

The Scripture, using the clearest possible language, forbids interest and its transactions. In fact, the Scripture goes one step beyond forbidding and actually declares war on those who insist on continuing in this practice and disregarding the laws of God.

Clearly, this is a most serious matter that is not to be taken lightly or overlooked!

Why Is Interest Forbidden?

"And for their taking of usury, while they were prohibited from doing so, and for their consuming the money of the people unjustly. We have prepared for the disbelievers among them a painful retribution." *(Qur'an 4:161)*

A study of interest using the tools of logic and reason will lead us to the foregone conclusion which the Scripture has already highlighted—the issue of injustice.

What has interest got to do with injustice?

Using simplified example, we will show how the injustice exists:

- We will take a small village, cut off from the world, and with a population of only 100 people.

- A wealthy villager has enough gold and silver to produce exactly 1,000 coins, and he convinces the villagers that to use these coins as a medium of exchange is easier than the barter system they had been engaged in.

- The wealthy villager (we will call him "the banker") lends his money in return for interest. So, for every ten coins he lends, he demands one extra coin in return as interest.

- Now, at the end of the loan period (assume it is one year), the banker goes to collect his money plus the interest. He finds that some villagers were successful through their work and trade in making the extra one coin, while others simply could not make the interest payment.

- The banker then confiscates the properties/ possessions of those villagers who defaulted. These properties/possessions are worth an amount at least equal to the money plus interest owed.

- Then, the banker starts the new year once again by lending out his 1,000 coins in return for interest, and the cycle goes on…

Though this example is extremely simplified, you may have been able to understand the design flaw related to the issue of interest. The flaw exists in that no matter how hard the villagers work, or how many goods they are able to produce, they will never all be able to meet the interest payment simply because only 1,000 coins exist, while the banker is waiting for 1,100 to be returned to him at the end of the year (hence it is a physical impossibility). This is why interest is forbidden in the Scripture and why God declares war on those who partake of it. It is a fraudulent system designed to trick people into giving up their possessions bit by bit until the bankers own everything and the free people become slaves on their own property!

Financial Institutions

The practices of financial institutions today warrant mention since they are not in conformity with the guidelines set out by the Scripture. Besides the issue of interest (which is covered in this chapter) there are some elements that need to be highlighted.

The Holding of Deposits

> *"And from among the people of the Book are those whom if you entrust him with a large amount he gives it back to you, and there are those whom if you entrust with one gold coin he will not return it to you unless you are standing over him. That is because they said: "We have no obligation towards the Gentiles." They say about God lies while they know." (Qur'an 3:75)*

The practice of banking today is based on the banks using the money of their customers to make loans or other financial transactions, thus becoming richer and richer without any benefit accruing to the owner of the money. This practice is akin to a person leaving his/her car at a parking garage only to have the car rented out by the attendants without the consent of the owner. If all the depositors were to come and withdraw their money at once (known as a run on the bank) they would be shocked to discover that the bank does not have their money and life savings available in its vaults as it has been lending and investing and even losing the money without the permission of the true owners of such money!

The financial institutions are not the owners of the money deposited with them, and therefore are not permitted under the Scripture to lend, invest, or otherwise utilize or benefit from such money without the full approval and consent of the money owner. Depositors would pay a fee to the financial institutions for ensuring the safekeeping of their money (by having vaults and security). Depositors would only receive payment from the financial institution if their money was being utilized and they were receiving a share of the profits (or loss) from such utilization.

Granting Credit Facilities

> *"O you who believe, if you borrow for a future period, then you shall record it. And let a scribe of justice record it for you; and let not the scribe refuse to record as God has taught him. Let him record and let the person who is borrowing dictate to him, and let him be aware of God, and let him not reduce from it anything. If the one who is borrowing is immature or weak or he cannot dictate himself, then let his guardian dictate with justice; and bring two witnesses from among your men; if there are not two men, then a man and two women from whom you will accept their testimony, so that if one of them becomes blindsided, then the one can remind the other. And let the witnesses not refuse to come if they are called. And do not fail to record it no matter how small or large until its maturity. That is more just with God and better for the testimony, and better that you do not have doubts; except if it is a trade to be done on the spot between you, then there is no sin upon you if you do not record it. And have evidence if you trade. No scribe shall be harmed nor any witness; for if you do so then it is a wickedness on your part, and be aware of God and God teaches you and God is aware of all things." (Qur'an 2:282)*

Lending is permitted for financial institutions on condition that there is no interest involved, and that the financial institution is lending its own money, or there is clear authorization from the owner of the money allowing such lending to take place.

There are alternative methods of financing that conform to the principles of the Qur'an and which will grant benefits/returns to the owners of the money while avoiding the injustice of interest:

Purchase Financing (Murabaha)

This is the method whereby the bank buys the goods on behalf of the customer and then sells it to the customer at a higher price over a longer period of time (e.g., the bank buys the house that Mrs. Adam wants for 100,000 Dinars and then sells it to Mrs. Adam for 120,000 Dinars over an installment period of 5 years). Although the goods or property would be given to the customer immediately, they would remain in the name/ownership of the bank as collateral until full payment is received.

The difference between this method and that of giving a direct loan that involves interest is threefold:

- There is no exchange of cash for more cash (this is the inherent flaw in the case of interest).

- The item remains the property of the seller until final payment is made.

- The price of the item is fixed (in this case at 120,000) with no possibility of increase even in cases of default (the deal may be called off, or the property confiscated and sold to another customer, but the price will not increase).

Investment Financing (Musharaka)

Investment Financing is the entering into partnership for a specific venture or company with each participant considered a part owner according to his/her share. Investment is a highly encouraged use of money as it not only creates wealth for the investor (if the venture is successful), but it also creates jobs and bolsters the economy through the circulation of money.

Development/Construction Financing (Istisn'a)

This method of financing is suitable for projects or goods that are yet to be developed/produced, but which the customer will be committed to purchasing once the deal is done. The bank would pay the contractor or developer directly and, once the project is complete, it would sell to the customer according to whatever terms and amounts were agreed prior to the development/construction.

Interest-free Loans

The bank may provide interest-free loans to its customers according to how it sees fit. Such loans may be collateralized partially or fully to remove any concern or doubt about repayment.

Credit Cards

Credit cards may be used in an Islamic based economy as long as the cardholder is not charged any interest. The way this can at the same time be profitable for the credit card companies is for retailers to agree to give a price "discount" to the credit card companies whenever their card is used to make a purchase. Thus, while an item may cost 100 Dinars to purchase in cash, the retailer would only bill the credit card company for 95 Dinars, while the credit card company bills the cardholder for the full price of 100 Dinars (the 5 Dinar becomes the revenue for the credit card company services).

The Buying and Selling of Foreign Currencies

"And it was thus that We delivered them so they would ask themselves. A speaker from among them said: 'How long have you stayed?' They said: 'We stayed a day or part of a day.' He said: 'Your Lord is surely aware how long you stayed, so send one of you with these stamped coins of yours to the city, and let

him see which is the tastiest food, and let him come with a provision of it. And let him be careful and let no one notice you.'" (Qur'an 18:19)

The buying and selling of foreign currencies is permitted on condition that the items being exchanged are of an equal value (i.e. money backed by gold and silver cannot be traded for a fiat note).

Land Ownership

"And remember that He made you successors after 'Aad, and He established you in the land so that you make palaces on its plains, and you carve homes in the mountains. So remember the grace of God, and do not roam the earth as corrupters." (Qur'an 7:74)

"And We let the people who were weak inherit the east of the land and the west of it which We have blessed. And the good word of your Lord was completed towards the Children of Israel for their patience; and We destroyed what Pharaoh and his people were doing, and what they contrived." (Qur'an 7:137)

Land may be owned by individuals or entities and may be traded, bought and sold. However, it is the duty of any Islamic government/state to ensure that the land is being developed or improved and that it is not simply trading hands for profit. This can be achieved through a system of penalties and fines which can be applied to residential areas to ensure that no land is being bought without there being a clear purpose and plan to develop and utilize it.

8

Environmental Protection

The Scripture places much focus on the issue of environmental protection, which includes the protection of both animals and the Earth. An evident attribute of a state that adheres to the Scripture would be its focus on the environment and ways in which the environment can be protected and the balance maintained.

> *"And He raised the heaven and He established the balance. Do not transgress in the balance."*
> *(Qur'an 55:7-8)*

The items listed are self-explanatory:

The Restricted Months

> *"O you who believe, honor your contracts. Made lawful for you are all the animals of the livestock, except that which is being recited to you. You are not permitted to hunt the game while you are under restriction. God decrees as He pleases." (Qur'an 5:1)*

> *"O you who believe, do not violate the symbols of God, nor the restricted month, nor the donations, nor what is regulated, nor the safety made by the Restricted Sanctuary; for they are seeking a bounty from their Lord and a blessing. And when it is permitted for you, then you may hunt. And let not the hatred of another people; because they had barred you from the Restricted Temple; make you aggress. And help each other in piety and righteousness, and do not help each other in sin and aggression. And be aware of God, for the retribution of God is severe." (Qur'an 5:2)*

> *"Lawful for you is the catch of the sea, to eat it as enjoyment for you and for those who travel; and unlawful for you is the catch of the land as long as you are under restriction; and be aware of God to whom you will be gathered." (Qur'an 5:96)*

Hunting Penalties

> *"O you who believe, do not kill any game while you are restricted; and whoever of you kills it deliberately, then the recompense is to value what was killed against the livestock, which shall be judged by two equitable persons from you, and to make it as a donation to reach the Base. Or, its expiation shall be*

91

in using it to feed the needy ones, while he abstains from it; that is to suffer the results of his deed; God forgives what has past. And whoever returns, then God will seek vengeance on him. God is Noble, capable of vengeance." (Qur'an 5:95)

"God has made the Base to be the Restricted Sanctuary; to enforce for the people, and for the restricted month, and for the donations, and for regulation; that is so you may know that God knows what is in the heavens and what is in earth, and that God is aware of all things." (Qur'an 5:97)

Restricted Foods

"Forbidden to you is that which is already dead, and the blood, and the meat of pig, and what was dedicated to other than God, and that which has been strangled, and that which has been beaten to death, and that which has fallen from a height, and that which has been gored, and that which the wild animals have eaten from except what you managed to rescue, and what has been slaughtered on altars, and what you divide by the arrows of chance. This is wickedness. Today the rejecters have given up from your system, so do not be concerned by them, but be concerned by Me. Today I have perfected your system for you, and completed My blessings upon you, and I have approved submission as the system for you. So, whoever is forced by severe hunger and not seeking sin, then God is Forgiving, Merciful." (Qur'an 5:3)

"They ask you what was made lawful to them, say: "All the good things have been made lawful for you, and what the trained dogs and birds catch, you teach

them from what God teaches you." So eat from what they have captured for you and mention the name of God upon it, and be aware of God. God is swift in reckoning." (Qur'an 5:4)

"Today, the good things have been made lawful to you, and the food of those who have been given the Book is lawful for you, and your food is lawful for them; and the independent females from those who are believers, and the independent females from those who have been given the Book before you, if you have given them their dowries, to be independent, not for illicit sex or taking lovers. And whoever rejects belief, then his work has fallen, and in the Hereafter he is of the losers." (Qur'an 5:5)

"So eat from that on which the name of God has been mentioned, if you indeed believe in His revelations. And why should you not eat that on which the name of God has been mentioned, when He has fully detailed to you what has been made unlawful; except what you are forced to? Many misguide by their desires without knowledge; your Lord is fully aware of the transgressors. And leave what is openly a sin and what is subtle of it; those who earn sin will be punished for what they have taken. And do not eat from that which the Name of God has not been mentioned, for it is wickedness. And the devils they inspire their supporters to argue with you; and if you obey them, then you are polytheists." (Qur'an 6:118-121)

Ecological Balance

"Have you noted the crops you reap? Did you grow them, or were We the Ones who grew them? If We wished, We can turn them into hay. Then you will be left in wonderment: 'We are lost. No, we are deprived!' Have you noted the water you drink? Did you send it down from the clouds, or was it We who sent it down? If We wished, We can make it salty. If only you would give thanks. Have you noted the fire you kindle? Did you establish its tree, or was it We who established it? We rendered it a reminder, and a useful tool for the users. You shall glorify the name of your Lord, the Great." (Qur'an 56:63-74)

"Until they came to a valley of ants, a female ant said: 'O ants, enter your homes else you will be crushed by Solomon and his soldiers while they do not notice.' He then smiled, amused by what she said. And he said: 'My Lord, help me to be thankful for the blessings You have bestowed upon me and upon my parents, and that I may do good works that pleases You, and admit me by Your Mercy with Your righteous servants.'" (Qur'an 27:18-19)

"Damage has appeared in the land and the sea at the hands of people by what they earn. He will make them taste some of what they have done, perhaps they will return." (Qur'an 30:41)

By neglecting our duties as a species and by abusing the natural environment, we risk damaging the habitat and home that God has made to provide for us until the Day of Judgment. It is only now in this century, after the damage has been done, that humankind understands the severity of these warnings.

9

Civil Laws

This chapter will deal with the laws of the Scripture regarding most (if not all) aspects of family, from marriage, family disputes, divorce proceedings, death and burial, to the handling of wills and inheritance.

Marriage

The following are the conditions to be met by people who are seeking marriage:

That the marriage is between a male and a female

"'Do you approach the males of the worlds? And you leave what your Lord has created for you of mates? You are an intrusive people!'" (Qur'an 26:165-166)

The male and female do not belong to the restricted groups

"And do not marry who your fathers had married from the women, except what has already been done. It is a lewdness, and an abhorrence, and an evil path. Forbidden for you are your mothers, and your daughters, and your sisters, and the sisters of your father, and the sisters of your mother, and the daughters of your brother, and the daughters of your sister, and your foster mothers who suckled you, and your sisters from suckling, and the mothers of your women, and your step-daughters who are in your lodgings from your women with whom you have already consummated the marriage; if you have not consummated the marriage then there is no sin upon you; and those who were in wedlock with your sons who are from your seed, and that you join between two sisters except what has already been done. God is Forgiving, Merciful. And the independent from the women, except those maintained by your oaths; the book of God over you; and permitted for you is what is beyond this, if you are seeking with your money to be independent, not for illicit sex. As for those whom you have already had joy with, then you shall give them their dowries as an obligation. There is no sin upon you for what you agree on after the obligation. God is Knowledgeable, Wise." (Qur'an 4:22-24)

"The divorce is allowed twice. So, either they remain

together equitably, or they part ways with goodness. And it is not lawful for you to take back anything you have given them unless you fear that they will not uphold the boundaries of God. So if you fear that they will not uphold the boundaries of God, then there is no sin upon them for what is given back. These are the boundaries of God so do not transgress them. And whoever shall transgress the boundaries of God, then these are the wicked. So if he divorces her again, then she will not be lawful for him until after she has married a different husband; if he divorces her; then there is no sin that they come back together if they think they will uphold the boundaries of God. These are the boundaries of God, He clarifies them for a people who know." (Qur'an 2:229-230)

That the male and female requesting marriage are single[4]

"And let those who are not able to marry continue to be chaste until God enriches them of His Bounty. And if those who are maintained by your oaths seek to consummate the marriage, then document it with them if you find that they are ready, and give them from the wealth of God which He has bestowed upon you. And do not force your daughters into marriage when they have desired independence, in order that you may make a gain in the goods of this worldly life. But if anyone has compelled them, then for their compulsion, God is Forgiving, Merciful." (Qur'an 24:33)

---

4 According to the Scripture in 4:3, an exception is allowed for a man to marry up to 4 wives if they are the mothers of orphans who are already under his care.

The male and female have parental consent if minors

"And whoever of you cannot afford to marry the independent female believers, then from those maintained by your oaths of the believing young women. And God is more aware of your faith, some of you to each other. You shall marry them with the permission of their parents and give them their dowries in kindness; to be independent, not for illicit sex or taking lovers. When they become independent, then any of them who come with lewdness shall have half of what is the punishment for those independent. This is for those who are concerned about deviating from among you. But if you are patient it is better for you, and God is Forgiver, Merciful." (Qur'an 4:25)

The male and female are of sound mind and not under duress

"And let those who are not able to marry continue to be chaste until God enriches them of His Bounty. And if those who are maintained by your oaths seek to consummate the marriage, then document it with them if you find that they are ready, and give them from the wealth of God which He has bestowed upon you. And do not force your daughters into marriage when they have desired independence, in order that you may make a gain in the goods of this worldly life. But if anyone has compelled them, then for their compulsion, God is Forgiving, Merciful." (Qur'an 24:33)

A dowry has been agreed upon and paid

"Today, the good things have been made lawful to you, and the food of those who have been given the

Book is lawful for you, and your food is lawful for them; and the independent females from those who are believers, and the independent females from those who have been given the Book before you, if you have given them their dowries, to be independent, not for illicit sex or taking lovers. And whoever rejects belief, then his work has fallen, and in the Hereafter he is of the losers." (Qur'an 5:5)

The man and woman are made aware of their obligations

"The men are to support the women with what God has bestowed upon them over one another and for what they spend of their money. The upright females are dutiful; keeping private the personal matters for what God keeps watch over. As for those females from whom you fear desertion, then you shall advise them, and abandon them in the bedchamber, and separate from them. If they respond to you, then do not seek a way over them; God is Most High, Great." (Qur'an 4:34)

The marriage is recorded

"And let those who are not able to marry continue to be chaste until God enriches them of His Bounty. And if those who are maintained by your oaths seek to consummate the marriage, then document it with them if you find that they are ready, and give them from the wealth of God which He has bestowed upon you. And do not force your daughters into marriage when they have desired independence, in order that you may make a gain in the goods of this worldly life. But if anyone

has compelled them, then for their compulsion, God is Forgiving, Merciful." (Qur'an 24:33)

Family Responsibility

"The men are to support the women with what God has bestowed upon them over one another and for what they spend of their money. The upright females are dutiful; keeping private the personal matters for what God keeps watch over. As for those females from whom you fear desertion, then you shall advise them, and abandon them in the bedchamber, and separate from them. If they respond to you, then do not seek a way over them; God is Most High, Great." (Qur'an 4:34)

Under the laws of the Scripture, the husband is required to provide for all expenses of the family unit (food, clothing, shelter, etc.) in keeping with his ability to do so.

Orphans

"And give the orphans their money, and do not replace the good with the bad, and do not consume their money with your money; for truly this is a great sin! And if you fear that you cannot be just to the orphans, then you may marry those who are agreeable to you of the women: two, and three, and four. But if you fear you will not be fair, then only one, or whom you maintain by your oaths. This is best that you do not face financial hardship. And give the women their dues willingly, and if they remit any of it to you of their own will, then you may take it with good feelings. And do not give the immature ones their money which God has entrusted to you, and spend on them from it and clothe them, and speak to them

in goodness. And test the orphans when they reach puberty, then, if you have determined from them comprehension, then give them their wealth, and do not deliberately consume it wastefully or quickly before they grow up. And whoever is rich, then let him not claim anything, and if he is poor then let him consume in kindness. If you give to them their wealth, then make a witness for them, and God is enough for Reckoning." (Qur'an 4:2-6)

Orphans are to be accommodated by the closest of kin, or by the state if there is no kin or if the kin is unwilling to take on this responsibly, until such time that they are deemed to have reached maturity. The money/inheritance of the orphan will be held in trust by the state until the orphan reaches adulthood. The custodian may request reimbursement from the trust fund for the cost of the accommodation and expenses of the orphan, provided the state is able to substantiate such claims.

Divorce Procedures

"And those divorced shall wait for three menstruation periods; and it is not lawful for them to conceal what God has created in their wombs, if they believe in God and the Last Day. And their husbands would then have just cause to return together, if they both wish to reconcile. And the obligations owed to them are to be fulfilled, as are the obligations owed by them. But the men will have a greater responsibility over them in this. And God is Noble, Wise." (Qur'an 2:228)

"The divorce is allowed twice. So, either they remain together equitably, or they part ways with goodness. And it is not lawful for you to take back anything you have given them unless you fear that they will

not uphold the boundaries of God. So if you fear that they will not uphold the boundaries of God, then there is no sin upon them for what is given back. These are the boundaries of God so do not transgress them. And whoever shall transgress the boundaries of God, then these are the wicked." (Qur'an 2:229)

"So if he divorces her again, then she will not be lawful for him until after she has married a different husband; if he divorces her; then there is no sin that they come back together if they think they will uphold the boundaries of God. These are the boundaries of God, He clarifies them for a people who know." (Qur'an 2:230)

"And if you have divorced the women, and they have reached their required interim period, then either you remain together equitably, or part ways equitably. And do not reconcile with them so you can harm them out of animosity; whoever does so is doing wrong to his soul; and do not take the revelations of God as mockery. And remember the blessings of God upon you, and what was sent down to you of the Book and the wisdom, He warns you with it. And be aware of God and know that God is Knowledgeable in all things." (Qur'an 2:231)

"And if you divorce the women, and they reach their required interim period, then do not make difficulty for them if they wish to remarry their husbands if they have amicably agreed among themselves out of what is best. This is to remind any of you who believe in God and the Last Day, this is better for you and purer; and God knows while you do not know." (Qur'an 2:232)

"O you who believe, if you marry the believing females, then divorce them before having intercourse with them, then there is no interim required of them. You shall compensate them, and let them go in an amicable manner." (Qur'an 33:49)

"O you prophet, if any of you have divorced the women, then they should be divorced while ensuring that their required interim is fulfilled, and keep count of the interim. You shall reverence God your Lord, and do not evict them from their homes, nor should they leave, unless they commit an evident lewdness. And these are the boundaries of God. And anyone who transgresses the boundaries of God has wronged his soul. You never know; perhaps God will make something come out of this." (Qur'an 65:1)

"Then, once the interim is fulfilled, either you remain together equitably, or part ways equitably and have it witnessed by two just people from among you; and give the testimony for God. This is to enlighten those who believe in God and the Last Day. And whoever reverences God, He will create a solution for him." (Qur'an 65:2)

"And He will provide for him whence he never expected. Anyone who puts his trust in God, then He suffices him. The commands of God will be done. God has decreed for everything its fate." (Qur'an 65:3)

"As for those who have reached menopause from your women, if you have any doubts, their interim shall be three months. And as for those whose menstruation has ceased, and those who are already pregnant, their interim is until they give birth. And anyone who

reverences God, He makes his matters easy for him."
(Qur'an 65:4)

"This is the command of God that He sends down to you. And anyone who is aware of God, He will forgive his sins, and will improve his reward." (Qur'an 65:5)

"You shall let them reside in the dwelling you were in when you were together, and do not coerce them to make them leave. And if they are pregnant, you shall spend on them until they give birth. Then, if they nurse the infant, you shall give them their due payment. And you shall maintain the amicable relations between you. If you disagree, then another woman may nurse the child." (Qur'an 65:6)

"O you who believe, if the believing females come emigrating to you, then you shall test them. God is fully aware of their belief. Thus, if you establish that they are believers, then you shall not return them to the disbelievers. They are no longer lawful for them, nor are the disbelievers lawful for them. And return the dowries that were paid. And there is no sin upon you to marry them, if you have paid their dowries to them. And do not keep disbelieving wives, and ask back what dowries you paid. And let them ask back what dowries they had paid. Such is the judgment of God; He judges between you. God is Knowledgeable, Wise." (Qur'an 60:10)

Summary of the Rules for Divorce:

- If they insist on divorce, then the wife and husband must remain together in the same home during the interim period. (65:1)

- If the couple reconcile, then divorce may be retracted and cancelled at any point during the interim period. (2:229)

- The divorce is automatically retracted if sexual intercourse takes place between the husband and wife during the interim period. (65:1)

- The interim period required is three menstruation periods. The interim for women who no longer menstruate is three months. The interim for pregnant women is until they deliver (2:228, 65:4)

- There is no interim period required if the divorce takes place before any sexual intercourse has taken place between the couple. (33:49)

- If the couple still wishes to follow through with the divorce after the end of the interim period, then two witnesses are required to complete the process. (65:2)

- If this is the third divorce, then the couple may not remarry each other unless the woman has been married to another man and then divorced. (2:230)

- A divorce may be forced, if there is just cause, where such may be granted by the court without an interim period. (60:10)

Husband and Wife Disputes

With regards to husband/wife disputes, the Qur'an gives us a list of remedies to attempt to save a marriage ranging from candor between the husband and wife, to temporary separation, to reconciliation through a mediator; with divorce being the very last resort.

> "And if a woman fears from her husband desertion or disregard, then there is no sin for them to reconcile

between themselves; and reconciliation is good. And the souls are brought by need. And if you are kind and do right, then God is expert over what you do." (Qur'an 4:128)

"The men are to support the women with what God has bestowed upon them over one another and for what they spend of their money. The upright females are dutiful; keeping private the personal matters for what God keeps watch over. As for those females from whom you fear desertion, then you shall advise them, and abandon them in the bedchamber, and separate from them. If they respond to you, then do not seek a way over them; God is Most High, Great." (Qur'an 4:34)

"And if you fear a permanent rift between them, then send a judge from his family and a judge from her family. If they want to reconcile, then God will bring them together. God is Knowledgeable, Expert." (Qur'an 4:35)

It is worth pointing out that verse 4:34 above has been traditionally interpreted in an incorrect manner by translating "idrib" as "beat/strike." This has caused terror to millions of Muslim women around the world for they fear that their husbands might beat them at will simply because they are dissatisfied or it suits their mood!

Some Arabic words, like in English, can have slightly different meanings depending on the context they are placed in. One such example is the word 'Daraba' which has a natural meaning of *putting forth* as can be seen in the following verses:

"Have you not seen how God puts forth (Daraba) the example that a good word is like a good tree, whose

root is firm and whose branches are in the heaven."
(Qur'an 14:24)

"For the poor who face hardship in the cause of God,
they cannot go forth (Darban) *in the land; the*
ignorant ones think they are rich from their modesty;
you know them by their features, they do not ask
the people repeatedly. And what you spend out of
goodness, God is fully aware of it." *(Qur'an 2:273)*

"O you who believe, if you go forth (Darabtum) *in the*
cause of God, you shall investigate carefully. And do
not say to those who greet you with peace: "You are not
a believer!" You are seeking the vanity of this world;
but with God are many riches. That is how you were
before, but God graced you, so investigate carefully.
God is expert over what you do." *(Qur'an 4:94)*

However, there are certain cases where this word can
have the meaning of 'strike/beat' as the act of striking
involves the hand being "put forth":

"So how will it be when their lives are terminated by
the angels, while striking (Yadriboona) *their faces*
and their backs?" (Qur'an 47:27)

The correct approach to the case of 4:34 is simply to
understand the *context* of the verse (in this case, it deals
with the subject of a woman who wishes to desert her
husband "Nushooz") and thus the word "Idribuhun" is one
of the suggested three steps suggested to deal with the
situation (the first step is talking it out, while the second is
giving her space by avoiding sexual contact with her).

"The men are to support the women with what God
has bestowed upon them over one another and for
what they spend of their money. The upright females

are dutiful; keeping private the personal matters for what God keeps watch over. As for those females from whom you fear desertion (Nushooz[5]), *then you shall advise them, and abandon them in the bedchamber, and separate from them* (Idribuhun). *If they respond to you, then do not seek a way over them; God is Most High, Great." (Qur'an 4:34)*

As such, which meaning of "Idribuhun" would make the most sense? Letting the wife temporarily separate from her husband and think things through, or, beating her into submission and forcing her to remain with her husband?

The answer is always to follow the *best* meaning derived...

"The ones who listen to what is being said, and then follow the best of it. These are the ones whom God has guided, and these are the ones who possess intelligence." (Qur'an 39:18)

Adopted Children

"God did not make any man with two hearts in his body. Nor did He make your wives whom you make estranged to be as your mothers. Nor did He make your adopted children to be your sons. Such is what you claim with your mouths, but God speaks the truth, and He guides to the path. Name them by their fathers. That is more just with God. But if you do not know their fathers, then, name them as your brothers in the system and your patrons. There is no sin upon you for what mistake you make in this respect; but you will be responsible for what your hearts deliberately intend. God is Forgiver, Merciful." (Qur'an 33:4-5)

---

5 Nushooz is correctly understood by translators as being 'leave/desert' as can be seen in its use in 4:128 and 58:11. However, miraculously, the word is transformed into 'ill-conduct' when the woman happens to be the one doing the Nushooz as in 4:34.

Children may be adopted based on the state ensuring that the family is suitable and is able to provide for the needs of the adopted child. Adopted children will retain their original family name even after adoption; they cannot carry the name of the adopting family.

Child Custody

> "And the divorced mothers are allowed to suckle their children two full years, if they wish to complete the suckling. And the man for whom the child is born is responsible for both their provisions and clothing equitably. A soul is not burdened except with what it can bear. No mother shall be harmed because of her child, nor shall a father be harmed because of his child. And for the guardian is the same requirement. So if they wish to separate out of mutual agreement and counsel, then there is no sin upon them. And if you want to hire nursing mothers, then there is no sin upon you if you return what you have been given equitably. And be aware of God, and know that God is watching over what you do." (Qur'an 2:233)

In cases of divorce or separation, the mother is entitled to the custody of the child up to the age of two years. For any children aged more than two years, the court will decide upon custody (either sole or joint) based on the ability and standing of each parent.

Death and Burial

> "So God sent forth a raven to scratch the land and show him how to deal with the body of his brother. He said: "Woe to me! Am I not even able to be like this raven and deal with the body of my brother?" So he became of those who regretted." (Qur'an 5:31)

"And the Hour is coming, there is no doubt in it, and God will resurrect those who are in the graves." (Qur'an 22:7)

Dead bodies are to be buried in the Earth within the shortest time-frame manageable. Bodies are not to be left to rot or decompose in the open causing a threat to the health of the living.

Inheritance and Wills

"It is decreed for you that if death should come to any of you, that it is best if he leaves a will for his family and relatives out of goodness; this is a truth for the righteous. Whoever alters it after having heard it, then the sin will be upon those who alter it. God is Hearer, Knowledgeable." (Qur'an 2:180-181)

"O you who believe, witnessing a will if death is approaching one of you shall be done by two who are just among you. Or, if you have gone forth in the land, then two others may suffice if death is approaching you; you will hold them after making the contact prayer, and they will swear by God if you have doubt: 'We will not purchase with it any price, even if he was a near relative, and we will not conceal the testimony of God, or else we are then of the sinners.' If it is then found out that they had lied, then two others will take their place from those who were present, and they will swear by God: 'Our testimony is more truthful than their testimony, and if we aggress, then we are of the wicked.' This is best so that they would bring the testimony on its face value, for fear that their oaths would be discarded after being made. And be aware of God, and listen; God does not guide the wicked people." (Qur'an 5:106-108)

"And for those of you whose lives are terminated and they leave widows behind; a testimony to them that they may enjoy for one year without being made to vacate. If they leave then there is no sin upon you for what they do to themselves in goodness; and God is Noble, Wise." (Qur'an 2:240)

"For the men is a portion from what the parents and the relatives left behind, and for the women is a portion from what the parents and relatives left behind, be it little or much; a forced portion. And if the distribution is attended by the relatives and the orphans and the needy, then you shall give them part of it and say to them a kind saying." (Qur'an 4:7-8)

"God directs you regarding the inheritance of your children: 'To the male shall be as that given to two females. If they are women, more than two, then they will have two thirds of what is inherited. And if she is only one, then she will have one half. And to his parents, each one of them shall have one sixth of what is inherited, if he has a child. If he has no child and his parents are the heirs, then to his mother is one third; if he has siblings then to his mother is one sixth. All after a will is carried through or a debt. Your parents and your children, you do not know which are closer to you in benefit, a directive from God, for God is Knowledgeable, Wise.' And for you is half of what your wives leave behind if they have no child; but if they have a child then to you is one quarter of what they leave behind. All after a will is carried through or a debt. And to them is one quarter of what you leave behind if you have no child; but if you have a child then to them is one eighth of what you leave behind. All after a will is carried through or a debt. And if a man or a woman who is inheriting has no descendants,

but has a brother or a sister, then to each one of them is one sixth, but if they are more than this then they are to share in one third. All after a will is carried through or a debt, which does not cause harm. A directive from God, and God is Knowledgeable, Compassionate." (Qur'an 4:11–12)

"They seek a ruling from you, say: 'God gives you the ruling for those who have no descendants. If a person passes away and has no children but has a sister, then she shall receive half of what he leaves behind. And he will inherit from her if she has no child. However, if he has two sisters, then they will receive two thirds of what he left behind; and if he has siblings, men and women, then the male shall receive twice what the female receives.' God makes clear to you that you do not stray; God is aware of all things." (Qur'an 4:176)

It is recommended that every person attempt to make a will and testament in writing before death to cover the distribution of property and wealth as he/she sees fit. A will that is not made in writing but has two credible witnesses may be enforceable, if the court is satisfied that their testimony is genuine.

In cases where there is no will and testament or if the will and testament leaves an amount of wealth undistributed, then the following distribution shall be applied to the available wealth:

- Due to the legal obligation of men to be responsible for their family, the inheritance as far as offspring is concerned entails the male receiving a share equal to that of two females, i.e., one girl = 1/3 and one boy = 2/3.

- If there are no males and there are two or more females, the portions of all of them together shall be 2/3; if there is one female, the portion shall be half.

- Parents receive one-sixth (1/6) of the inheritance each, in the case where the deceased has left children. If there are no children and the parents are the only heirs, the share of the mother shall be 1/3 and that of the father share shall be 2/3. If the deceased left brothers and sisters, the share of the mother is 1/6.

- In what a wife leaves, the share of the husband is one-half in the case where she leaves no children; but if she has children, then the share of the husband is 1/4 after the processing of the will and the payment of debt against the deceased.

- In what a husband leaves, the share of the wife is 1/4, if he has no children, but if he has children, the share of the wife is 1/8 after the processing of the will and payment of debt against the deceased.

- If the deceased has no children but he has parents, brothers and sisters, then:

  - If there is one brother or one sister, each one of them shall receive 1/6;

  - If the number of brothers and sisters is more than one, then together they shall be entitled to 1/3.

- If the deceased has neither children nor living parents but has only brothers and sisters, the distribution of shares shall be as per the following:

  - If the deceased is a male, and has only one sister, then her portion shall be half of his bequest;

- If the deceased is a female, and has only one brother, then he shall be the heir of her leftover property;

- If the heirs are two sisters (or more), their (combined) share shall be 2/3;

- If the heirs are brothers and sisters, then the entire leftover property shall be theirs. The principle of "the share of two females is equal to the share of one male" shall apply.

Any property or wealth that still remains after the distribution as per the guidelines above shall be transferred to the state.

10

Commercial Laws

This chapter will deal with all legal aspects of commerce, trade and financial transactions.

Breach of Contract

> *"O you who believe, honor your contracts. Made lawful for you are all the animals of the livestock, except that which is being recited to you. You are not permitted to hunt the game while you are under restriction. God decrees as He pleases." (Qur'an 5:1)*

Breach of contract will result in the guilty party being ordered to complete the contract as agreed or to compensate the other contract party for damages incurred by such breach.

Drug/Alcohol

It is worth noting that neither using nor manufacturing alcohol is forbidden in the Scripture. In fact, alcohol has been recognized casually in the Scripture in several verses, even to the point of relating it to the conduct of Salat and that one should not approach Salat if intoxicated.

> "And from the fruits of the palm trees and the grapes you make wine and a good provision. In that is a sign for a people who comprehend." (Qur'an 16:67)

> "Is the example of the Paradise; that the righteous have been promised with rivers of pure water, and rivers of milk whose taste does not change, and rivers of wine that are delicious for the drinkers, and rivers of strained honey, and for them in it are all kinds of fruits, and a forgiveness from their Lord; like that of those who abide in the Fire, and are given to drink boiling water that cuts-up their intestines?" (Qur'an 47:15)

> "O you who believe, do not approach the contact prayer (Salat) while you are intoxicated, until you know what you are saying. Nor if you have had intercourse, unless traveling, until you bathe. And if you are ill, or traveling, or one of you has excreted feces, or you had sexual contact with the women, and could not find water, then you shall select from the clean soil; you shall wipe your faces and hands. God is Pardoning, Forgiving." (Qur'an 4:43)

The scholars attribute the inconsistency in their understanding of the issue (they believe alcohol is forbidden) to say that God, while not having any problem tearing the social fabric of their society and lives, did not forbid alcohol outright for fear that people would not embrace Islam during its early days; but that when Islam had spread, the Scripture required people to 'avoid/shun' alcohol based on the verse below:

> *[Shakir Translation 5:90] "O you who believe! Intoxicants and games of chance and (sacrificing to) stones set up and (dividing by) arrows are only an uncleanness, the Shaitan's work; shun it therefore that you may be successful."*

Of course, the attempt to prove that there may be inconsistencies or conflicting laws in the Scripture falls on its face when the verse is examined closely... In verse 5:90, the thing we are being told to "avoid" is not alcohol or any of the other listed items (i.e. they are not to be shunned/avoided in themselves), rather it is *the devil* himself whom we should avoid and we must be aware that his tools of preference for creating animosity and addiction to our species includes, amongst other things, alcohol.

> *"O you who believe, intoxicants, and gambling, and sacraments, and fortunes are an affliction used by the devil. You shall avoid him so that you may be successful." (Qur'an 5:90)*

This reference to the 'Devil' and not the items listed can be very clearly seen in the very next verse that emphasizes on the subject matter once again being the 'Devil':

> *"The devil only wants to cause strife between you through intoxicants and gambling, and to repel you away from remembering God and from the contact prayer. Will you be deterred?" (Qur'an 5:91)*

This is similar to the situation where our children and wealth could be a distraction to us from remembering God. This does not mean that our children and wealth are 'evil' and need to be shunned or avoided or forbidden, but that we need to be more aware and responsible as to how we spend our time:

> "O you who believe, do not be distracted by your money and your children from the remembrance of God. And those who do this, then they are the losers." (Qur'an 63:9)

Finally, while alcohol is clearly not forbidden, its use is to be restricted and regulated since there can be more harm that good in their unabated use/consumption.

> "They ask you about intoxicants and gambling. Say: "In them is great harm, and a benefit for the people; but their harm is greater than their benefit." And they ask you how much they are to give, say: "The excess." It is thus that God clarifies for you the revelations that you may think." (Qur'an 2:219)

Plagiarism

> "Do not think that those who are happy with what they have been given, and they love to be praised for what they did not do; do not think they are saved from the punishment. For them is a painful retribution." (Qur'an 3:188)

The use or benefit from the work of others without permission and/or acknowledgement is an abhorrent act and may be regulated or have legal penalties imposed by the state.

Property Disputes

> "When they entered upon David, he was startled
> by them. They said: "Have no fear. We are two
> who have disputed, and one has wronged the other,
> so judge between us with the truth, and do not
> wrong us, and guide us to the right path. This is
> my brother and he owns ninety-nine lambs, while
> I own one lamb; so he said to me: 'Let me take
> care of it' and he pressured me.'" He said: 'He has
> wronged you by asking to combine your lamb with
> his lambs. And many who mix their properties take
> advantage of one another, except those who believe
> and do good works, and these are very few.' And
> David guessed that We had tested him, so he sought
> forgiveness from his Lord, and fell down kneeling,
> and repented." (Qur'an 38:22-24)

The owner of the property or goods by way of title
deed or witnesses shall be returned his/her property. In
case where the property is being used or occupied, then
such property shall be vacated and returned to its legal
owner(s).

Property Damage

> "And David and Solomon, when they gave judgment
> in the case of the crop that was damaged by the sheep
> of the people, and We were witness to their judgment."
> (Qur'an 21:78)

The owner of the property shall be compensated in
full either by money or property/goods of an equivalent
nature and value.

Financial Interest

> "Those who consume usury do not rise except as one being influenced by the touch of the devil. That is because they have said: "Trade is the same as usury." While God has made trade lawful, and He has made usury unlawful. Whoever has received understanding from His Lord and ceases, then he will be forgiven for what was before this and his case will be with God. But whoever returns, then they are the people of the Fire, in it they will abide." (Qur'an 2:275)

Under no condition whatsoever will the charging or paying of interest on money be allowed. The concept of interest involves deceit and fraud, which will lead to financial hardship and cheating people out of their possessions. Any individuals found guilty of taking interest on money directly or indirectly (even with the consent of all parties involved) will be subject to the full extent of the law, and the court may find transactions or contracts with interest built-in null and void.

Borrowing Laws

> "O you who believe, if you borrow for a future period, then you shall record it. And let a scribe of justice record it for you; and let not the scribe refuse to record as God has taught him. Let him record and let the person who is borrowing dictate to him, and let him be aware of God, and let him not reduce from it anything. If the one who is borrowing is immature or weak or he cannot dictate himself, then let his guardian dictate with justice; and bring two witnesses from among your men; if there are not two men, then a man and two women from whom you will accept their testimony, so that if one of them becomes blindsided, then the one can remind the other. And let the witnesses not refuse to come if they are called.

And do not fail to record it no matter how small or large until its maturity. That is more just with God and better for the testimony, and better that you do not have doubts; except if it is a trade to be done on the spot between you, then there is no sin upon you if you do not record it. And have evidence if you trade. No scribe shall be harmed nor any witness; for if you do so then it is a wickedness on your part, and be aware of God and God teaches you and God is aware of all things." (Qur'an 2:282)

The lending of money is permitted as long as there is no hidden or evident interest involved. All borrowing contracts must be recorded in writing (even if it is between relatives) with the dictation of the details being provided by the person borrowing the money.

Witnessing shall be required if the money is being borrowed by a legally authorized third party or guardian on behalf of the original borrower. These measures are to be made to ensure the rights of both parties are protected and that the transaction being conducted is genuine and involves no fraud or deceit.

Insolvency

"If the person is facing insolvency, then you shall wait until he becomes able. And if you relinquish it as a charity it is better for you if only you knew.." (Qur'an 2:280)

Individuals and companies may file for insolvency if such claim can be substantiated. Once an individual or company has been approved as being insolvent, then all creditors/lenders must restructure their repayment tenor in line with what is realistic and manageable for the insolvent party.

11

Criminal Laws

This chapter will deal with all legal aspects of criminal activity and/or behavior. All court trials and judges are to observe the following guidelines:

Inadmissible Evidence

> *"And do not uphold what you have no knowledge of. For the hearing, eyesight, and mind, all these you are responsible for." (Qur'an 17:36)*

Testimony can only be given for what was witnessed first-hand. Hearsay is inadmissible in a court of law.

Seek Clarifications

"O you who believe, if a wicked person comes to you with any news, then you shall investigate it. Lest you harm a people out of ignorance, then you will become regretful over what you have done." (Qur'an 49:6)

The court is required to thoroughly investigate all cases and claims that come to its attention and to examine all sides of a case before passing judgment.

Everybody Shall Bear His/Her Own Burden

"None can carry the burdens of another." (Qur'an 53:38)

The court is forbidden from making charges or issuing a punishment against any other than the convicted person(s). Family members, relatives, friends, associates, or any other person (even if volunteering to do so) are protected from undue punishment and may not be traded for the convicted person nor may they take his/her place.

State of the Accused

"There is no blame upon the blind, nor is there any blame upon the crippled, nor is there any blame upon the ill, nor is there any blame upon yourselves, if you eat at your homes, or the homes of your fathers, or the homes of your mothers, or the homes of your brothers, or the homes of your sisters, or the homes of your uncles, or the homes of your aunts, or the homes of your mothers brothers, or the homes of your mothers sisters, or that which you possess their keys, or that of your friends. You commit nothing wrong by eating together or as individuals. When you enter any home,

123

you shall greet each other a greeting from God that is
blessed and good. God thus explains the revelations
for you that you may comprehend." (Qur'an 24:61)

The court is to take into account and use its judgment regarding the physical and mental state of the accused. Actions committed by a fully competent and able adult are not the same as those committed by a person who is mentally ill or suffering from a temporary illness/insanity.

Bearing Witness

"O you who believe, stand with justice as witnesses
to God, even if against yourselves, or the parents or
the relatives. Even if he be rich or poor, God is more
worthy of them, so do not follow desire into being
unjust. And if you twist or turn away, then God is
Expert over what you do." (Qur'an 4:135)

"O you who believe, if you borrow for a future period,
then you shall record it. And let a scribe of justice record
it for you; and let not the scribe refuse to record as God
has taught him. Let him record and let the person who is
borrowing dictate to him, and let him be aware of God,
and let him not reduce from it anything. If the one who
is borrowing is immature or weak or he cannot dictate
himself, then let his guardian dictate with justice; and
bring two witnesses from among your men; if there
are not two men, then a man and two women from
whom you will accept their testimony, so that if one of
them becomes blindsided, then the one can remind the
other. And let the witnesses not refuse to come if they
are called. And do not fail to record it no matter how
small or large until its maturity. That is more just with
God and better for the testimony, and better that you
do not have doubts; except if it is a trade to be done on

the spot between you, then there is no sin upon you if you do not record it. And have evidence if you trade. No scribe shall be harmed nor any witness; for if you do so then it is a wickedness on your part, and be aware of God and God teaches you and God is aware of all things." (Qur'an 2:282)

Witnesses cannot be harmed in any way as a result of their testimony. This includes being forced to be a witness against him/herself. Witnesses must present themselves when required to do so by the court and may not refuse to give testimony of what they have witnessed. The court may take the appropriate action against witnesses that refuse to give testimony (unless it is against themselves).

Confessions of Guilt

"He said: 'Did we not raise you among us as a new born, and you stayed with us for many of your years? And you did what deed you did, and you are of the rejecters.' He said: 'I did it, and I was of those misguided.'" (Qur'an 26:18-20)

"Whoever rejects God after having believed; except for he who is forced while his heart is still content with belief; and has comforted his chest to rejection, then these will have a wrath from God and they will have a great retribution." (Qur'an 16:106)

Confessions are admissible in court provided the accused person directly makes them without duress or intimidation. Confessions under duress or intimidation or not spoken directly by the accused are considered invalid and may not be used to pass judgment with.

False Accusations

> "O you who believe, if a wicked person comes to you
> with any news, then you shall investigate it. Lest you
> harm a people out of ignorance, then you will become
> regretful over what you have done." (Qur'an 49:6)

False accusations or lodging of fabricated evidence
or testimony grants the court the right to prosecute
the party involved in such activity either through
fine or imprisonment depending on the scope of the
accusations made.

Sanctity of the Home and Personal Property

> "O you who believe, do not enter any homes except
> your own unless you perceive a welcome and you
> greet the people in them. This is best for you, perhaps
> you will remember. But, if you do not find anyone
> in them then do not enter until you are given
> permission. And if you are told to go back, then
> return for it is better for you. And God is aware
> of what you do. There is no sin upon you that you
> enter homes which are abandoned if in them there
> are belongings of yours. And God knows what you
> reveal and what you hold back." (Qur'an 24:27-29)

Evidence obtained from a residential home without
the consent of the owner, or a court order, is inadmissible
as evidence.

Injunction against Spying

> "O you who believe, you shall avoid much suspicion,
> for some suspicion is sinful. And do not spy on one
> another, nor shall you backbite. Would any of you
> enjoy eating the flesh of his dead brother? You

certainly would hate this. You shall observe God. God is Redeemer, Merciful." (Qur'an 49:12)

Evidence obtained through spying or eavesdropping is inadmissible in a court of law.

Juveniles and Young Adults

"O mankind, if you are in doubt as to the resurrection, then We have created you from dust, then from a seed, then from an embryo, then from a fetus developed and undeveloped so that We make it clear to you. And We settle in the wombs what We wish to an appointed time, then We bring you out a child, then you reach your maturity, and of you are those who will pass away, and of you are those who are sent to an old age where he will not be able to learn any new knowledge after what he already has. And you see the land still, but when We send down the water to it, it vibrates and grows, and it brings forth of every lovely pair." (Qur'an 22:5)

"And whoever of you cannot afford to marry the independent female believers, then from those maintained by your oaths of the believing young women. And God is more aware of your faith, some of you to each other. You shall marry them with the permission of their parents and give them their dowries in kindness; to be independent, not for illicit sex or taking lovers. When they become independent, then any of them who come with lewdness shall have half of what is the punishment for those independent. This is for those who are concerned about deviating from among you. But if you are patient it is better for you, and God is Forgiver, Merciful." (Qur'an 4:25)

The court is to take the age of the accused person into account when issuing judgments. All youths will be transferred automatically to the juvenile court. Young people and mature adults are never to be treated as the same in issuing judgment. In the example given in 4:25 above, a young adult who commits adultery will receive half the punishment of a mature adult (i.e., 50 lashes).

Prisons

> "And with him in the prison entered two young men. One of them said: 'I dreamt that I was pressing wine,' and the other said: 'I dreamt that I was carrying bread on top of my head, and that the birds were eating from it.' 'Tell us what this means, for we see that you are of the good doers.'" (Qur'an 12:36)

Prisoners are to be held in groups of three or less depending on the circumstances. Prisoners are to be provided adequate food, water, clothing and medical treatment. Visitations to prisoners are allowed in conformity with the schedules to be set out by the state. Prisoners are to be given ample opportunity for study, education, learning of crafts/skills, etc., to positively utilize time spent in prison. Prisoners are to be treated humanely and with respect at all times. No abuse, torture, physical pain nor suffering is allowed at any time.

Crimes and Judgments

Below are guidelines for criminal rulings based on key offenses. Other offenses that are not listed will be judged based on the principle of equitable punishment (16:126).

Murder/Violence

> "And We have decreed for them in it that a life for a life, and an eye for an eye, and a nose for a nose,

> *and an ear for an ear, and a tooth for a tooth, and
> wounds to be similar; and whoever remits anything
> of it, then it will cancel sins for him. And whoever
> does not judge with what God has sent down, then
> these are the wicked." (Qur'an 5:45)*

The court may physically punish the accused up to the
same level of the physical crime committed. Murder is met
with execution, and a cut is met with a cut. However, the
person or family of the person who has been harmed may
remit the punishment in part or in full. Such remittance of
punishment will override the court ruling on this matter.

Accidental Death

> *"And it is not for a believer to kill another believer
> except by mistake. And whoever kills a believer by
> mistake, then he shall free a believing slave, and give
> compensation to the family; except if they remit it. If he
> was from a people who are enemies to you, and he was
> a believer, then you shall free a believing slave. And if
> he was from a people with whom you have a covenant,
> then a compensation to his family, and free a believing
> slave. Whoever does not find, then the fasting of two
> months sequentially as a repentance from God; for God
> is Knowledgeable, Wise." (Qur'an 4:92)*

Accidental death (manslaughter) must be met with:
a) freeing of any believing slave, b) giving financial
compensation to the family of the victim. The financial
compensation may only be withheld if the family of the
victim cannot be reached due to hostility or war being waged
between the respective nations, or if the family remits the
compensation. If slaves to be freed are not found, then the
ruling shall be for the accused to fast for two consecutive
months (60 days) from sunrise until night.

Suicide

> "O you who believe, do not consume your money between you unjustly, unless it is through a trade which is mutually agreed by you. And do not kill yourselves; God is Merciful towards you. And whoever does so out of animosity and transgression, We will cast him to a Fire; and this for God is very easy." (Qur'an 4:29-30)

The law prohibits suicide if it is being done as an act of despair against God or from life (i.e. being done out of "animosity, or transgression"). Any person found guilty of attempting suicide must be professionally counseled or restrained until the court sees the threat of suicide is no longer present.

Abortion

> "Say: 'Come let me recite what your Lord has made unlawful for you: that you should not set up anything with Him; and do good to your parents; and do not kill your children for fear of poverty, We provide for you and for them; and do not come near lewdness, what is openly of it and what is subtle; and do not kill the soul which God has made restricted, except in justice. That is what He enjoined you that you may comprehend.'" (Qur'an 6:151)

> "And We enjoined the human being to do good to his parents. His mother bore him with hardship, gave birth to him in hardship, and his bearing and weaning lasts thirty months. So that, when he has reached his independence, and he has reached forty years, he says: 'My Lord, direct me to appreciate the blessings You have bestowed upon me and upon my parents, and to do good work that pleases You. And

*let my progeny be righteous. I have repented to You;
I am of those who have submitted."' (Qur'an 46:15)*

*"And We enjoined the human being regarding his
parents. His mother bore him with hardship upon
hardship, and his weaning takes two years. You shall
give thanks to Me, and to your parents. To Me is the
final destiny." (Qur'an 31:14)*

In looking to the above verses, specifically in 46:15
that the bearing and weaning of a child takes 30 months,
and then in 31:14 that identifies the weaning as a period
of two years (i.e. 24 months), that will leave us with a
difference of 6 months in which the child is to be carried
in pregnancy. Therefore, and since a natural pregnancy
cycle is 9 months, this implies that in the first 3 months
the fetus is not yet considered a child.

As such, abortion is only permitted if the fetus is less
than three months old, or, if there is a clear threat to the
life of the pregnant mother. Other than this, abortion is
considered a sinful act which is to be discouraged.

Rebellion/Spying/Espionage

*"The recompense of those who fight God and His
messenger, and seek to make corruption in the land, is
that they will be killed or crucified or that their hands
and feet be cut off from alternate sides or that they be
banished from the land; that is a disgrace for them in
this world and in the Hereafter they will have a great
retribution. Except for those who repent before you
overpower them, then know that God is Forgiving,
Merciful." (Qur'an 5:33–34)*

Any person convicted of endangering the lives of
citizens through espionage, spying, sedition, incitement of
violence or mutiny will be liable to the full extent of the

law as determined by the court ranging from execution to amputation of alternate limbs and to deportation from the land. However, an exception exists for those who surrender themselves willingly to the state before being found or captured and repent from their actions. Such cases will not be subject to the penalties of rebellion but are subject to the penalties of equivalence for any crimes committed.

Slavery

> "Do you know which is the better path? The freeing of slaves." (Qur'an 90:12-13)

Any attempt made to own or enslave a human being (even with the consent of the person enslaved) is completely forbidden. Persons owning slaves are encouraged to set them free as an act of righteousness and brotherhood.

Indecent Exposure and Pornography

> "O Children of Adam, We have sent down for you garments to alleviate your sin, and feathers; and the garment of righteousness is the best. That is from the signs of God, perhaps they will remember." (Qur'an 7:26)

> "And tell the believing females to lower their gaze and keep covered their private parts, and that they should not reveal their beauty except what is apparent, and let them put forth their shawls over their cleavage. And let them not reveal their beauty except to their husbands, or their fathers, or fathers of their husbands, or their sons, or the sons of their husbands, or their brothers, or the sons of their brothers, or the sons of their sisters, or their women, or those maintained by their oaths, or the male servants who are without need, or the child who has not yet understood the composition of women. And

let them not strike with their feet in a manner that reveals what they are keeping hidden of their beauty. And repent to God, all of you believers, that you may succeed." (Qur'an 24:31)

The minimum legal requirement for public display is that men and women both cover their lower private parts (genitalia, buttocks), in addition to women covering their breasts.

Adultery

"The adulteress and the adulterer, you shall lash each of them with one hundred lashes, and do not let any pity overtake you regarding the system of God if you believe in God and the Last Day. And let a group of the believers witness their punishment. The adulterer will only marry an adulteress or she who is a polytheist. And the adulteress, she will only be married to an adulterer or he who is a polytheist. And such has been made unlawful upon the believers. And those who accuse the independent females and they do not bring forth four witnesses, then you shall lash them eighty lashes and do not ever accept their testimony; and those are the wicked. Except those who repent after this and do good, then God is Forgiving, Merciful." (Qur'an 24:2-5)

"And whoever of you cannot afford to marry the independent female believers, then from those maintained by your oaths of the believing young women. And God is more aware of your faith, some of you to each other. You shall marry them with the permission of their parents and give them their dowries in kindness; to be independent, not for illicit sex or taking lovers. When they become

independent, then any of them who come with lewdness shall have half of what is the punishment for those independent. This is for those who are concerned about deviating from among you. But if you are patient it is better for you, and God is Forgiver, Merciful." (Qur'an 4:25)

"And those of your women who commit lewdness, you shall bring four witnesses over them from among you; if they bear witness, then you shall restrict them in the homes until death terminates their lives, or God makes for them a way out." (Qur'an 4:15)

Adultery is the act of sexual intercourse between a man and woman who are not married to one another. Any accusation of adultery will not be accepted unless four eyewitnesses are produced to support the adultery charges. The witnesses must have seen the act of sexual intercourse first-hand (hearsay, circumstantial or any other non-direct evidence will not be accepted). In case four true witnesses are presented, then the court will issue the required sentence of 100 lashes for the man and 100 lashes for the woman involved in the adultery if the woman is independent/mature, or 50 lashes for the woman if she is married but not yet independent/mature, or, house arrest for the woman if she is unmarried and not independent/mature. The lashings must be publicly witnessed to cause embarrassment to the guilty parties.

In case four witness are not presented or the witnesses are not all found to be true, then the person who brought forth the accusation and the persons who gave false testimony will be lashed 80 lashes each and will be refused future testimonies with the court unless they have repented.

Accusations of Adultery by Husband/Wife

> *"And those who accuse their spouses, but they have no witnesses except for themselves, then the testimony of one of them is to be equivalent to that of four witnesses if it is sworn by God that they are being truthful. And the fifth shall be the curse of God upon themselves if they are of the liars." (Qur'an 24:6-7)*

> *"And the punishment will be averted from her if she bears witness four times by God that he is of the liars. And the fifth shall be the curse of God upon her if he is speaking the truth." (Qur'an 24:8-9)*

A man or woman may accuse his/her spouse of adultery in court without having any witnesses except themselves if they swear an oath by God four times to such effect. However, in cases of the husband accusing his wife, she will be able to counter and nullify his accusation if she swears an oath by God four times that he is lying.

The punishment in such case of adultery would be 100 lashes in public, or 50 lashes for the woman if she is not yet independent/mature.

Sexual Molestation and Rape

> *"And as they rushed towards the door, she tore his shirt from behind; and they found her master at the door. She said: 'What is the punishment for he who wanted evil for your family? Is it not that he be imprisoned or punished painfully?'" (Qur'an 12:25)*

> *"And he said to the one whom he thought would be saved of them: "Mention me to your lord." But the devil made him forget to mention to his lord, so He remained in prison for a few years." (Qur'an 12:42)*

Cases of sexual molestation or rape if proven to be accurate will carry either a prison sentence (not to exceed five years based on the example of 12:42) and/or a physical punishment as determined by the court (the physical punishment may not be excessive to the nature of the crime committed).

Homosexuality

> *"And the two men who commit it from among you, you shall trouble them. If they repent and amend, then leave them alone. God is Redeemer, Merciful."* (Qur'an 4:16)

Homosexuality shall be discouraged by the means that the court sees fit, with the intent to repel such individuals from engaging in homosexual acts. Sentence shall be suspended in case the accused repents from such activity.

Theft/Financial Fraud

> *"As for the thief, both male and female, you shall cut from their resources – as a penalty for what they have earned – to be made an example of from God. God is Noble, Wise."* (Qur'an 5:38)

In cases of proven theft, the court shall order the return of the stolen item(s)/good(s)/property as well as their equivalent value. In cases where no such goods or resources are available, then the penalty shall be to hold the thief in custody and sentencing him/her to labor at a fair market price. Money raised from the work shall serve to compensate the state or the person(s) from whom the theft occurred.

Bribery

> *"As for the thief, both male and female, you shall cut*

from their resources – as a penalty for what they have earned – to be made an example of from God. God is Noble, Wise." (Qur'an 2:188)

Paying bribes to employees in government or otherwise will result in the court taking immediate action against the person making the bribe through confiscation of the bribe amount, and/or the imposing of a fine and/or sentencing the person to a prison sentence as determined appropriate by the court Judge.

Disturbing the Peace

"'And be humble in how you walk and lower your voice. For the harshest of all voices is the voice of the donkeys.'" (Qur'an 31:19)

Disturbance of the peace, if proven to be excessive, may result in action to be specified by the court.

Negligence and Impeachment

"O you who believe, do not betray God and the messenger, nor betray your trust, while you know." (Qur'an 8:27)

"It was not for any prophet to embezzle, and he who embezzles will be brought with what he has embezzled on the Day of Resurrection, then every soul will be given what it has earned without being wronged." (Qur'an 3:161)

All employees and officials are fully accountable for their position and all the responsibilities and duties entailed therein. People who betray the trust of office may be removed from office, fined or imprisoned by the court.

12

Rules of Warfare

This chapter will outline the rules that regulate and determine warfare from the Scripture as well as the structure and scope of military campaigns/operations.

> *"Warfare has been decreed for you while you hate it; and perhaps you may hate something while it is good for you, and perhaps you may love something while it is bad for you; and God knows while you do not know." (Qur'an 2:216)*

Establishing an Army

> *"And prepare for them all that you can of might, and from the steeds of war, that you may instill terror with it towards the enemy of God and your enemy, and others besides them whom you do not know but God knows them. And whatever you spend in the cause of God will be returned to you, and you will not be wronged." (Qur'an 8:60)*

Establishing an army is a requirement of any Islamic state in order to defend its people, property and constitution. Not having a military force is an invitation for invasion or some disaster lying in wait at some future point.

Military Service

> *"O prophet, urge the believers to fight. If there are twenty of you who are patient, they will defeat two hundred. And if there are one hundred of you, they will defeat one thousand from among those who reject; that is because they are a people who do not understand." (Qur'an 8:65)*

The army shall be made up of men and women who render such a service of their own free will and under no compulsion whatsoever. These individuals are to be provided a wage and other benefits and services as established by the state. In wartime, the state may call on able-bodied men and women who upon their own freewill are ready to form militias to defend the state and its citizens.

Defensive Warfare

> *"And fight in the cause of God against those who fight you, but do not aggress, God does not love the aggressors. And kill them wherever you overcome them, and expel them from where they expelled you,*

*and know that persecution is worse than being killed.
And do not fight them at the Restricted Temple
unless they fight you in it; if they fight you then kill
them, thus is the recompense of the disbelievers. And
if they cease, then God is Forgiving, Merciful. And
fight them so there is no more persecution, and so
that the system is for God. If they cease, then there
will be no aggression except against the wicked."
(Qur'an 2:190–193)*

This is where the territory of the state has come
under direct attack or threat of attack. In such a case, the
Scripture grants automatic authority to conduct full-battle
mobilization and to conduct defensive strikes in retaliation
to the attacks incurred. Warfare in this scenario is to be
conducted until the invading force(s) is driven back, if they
cease and withdraw, or if they completely surrender.

If any part of the state has fallen under occupation, then
no treaties, negotiations, or ceasefires may be entered into until
the enemy has surrendered or has been fully driven out
from the lands and locations occupied. Any such treaties
or negotiations entered into on behalf of the state while
under occupation shall be considered null and void.

Under such warfare, the categorization of enemies
becomes as follows:

Invading Soldiers, Special Forces, Mercenaries, and Various Armed Units

*"And fight in the cause of God against those who
fight you, but do not aggress, God does not love the
aggressors. And kill them wherever you overcome
them, and expel them from where they expelled you,
and know that persecution is worse than being killed.
And do not fight them at the Restricted Temple
unless they fight you in it; if they fight you then kill*

them, thus is the recompense of the disbelievers."
(Qur'an 2:190-191)

Invading soldiers and all armed forces/units that support them may be attacked, fought, and killed whenever and wherever they are found unless they surrender or completely withdraw from the areas they have invaded.

Occupation Installed Army or Policing Force (i.e. Puppet Police or Army)

"You will find others who want to be safe among you and safe among their own people. Every time they are returned to the test, they fall back in it. If they do not withdraw from you, and offer you peace, and restrain their hands, then you shall take them and kill them wherever you overcome them. For these We have given you a clear authority." (Qur'an 4:91)

Although these people are normally citizens of the invaded country/nation, they are considered to be an extension of the invading army as they offer support, intelligence, and protection to the invader. Invading armies typically use these local militias or army formations as a 'front line' to defend them from attacks or to have them search out and kill or capture defenders.

Such people are to be fought and killed without hesitation until they cease their actions of support for the invading army.

Traitors, Spies, and Collaborators

"The recompense of those who fight God and His messenger, and seek to make corruption in the land, is that they will be killed or crucified or that their hands and feet be cut off from alternate sides or that they be banished from the land; that is a disgrace for them in

141

this world and in the Hereafter they will have a great
retribution. Except for those who repent before you
overpower them, then know that God is Forgiving,
Merciful." (Qur'an 5:33-34)

This section of people is the most vile. They mingle
with the people as if they are with them, but then would
pass on information to the invaders regarding formations,
weapons, readiness, battle plans and locations. This group
by far causes the most set-backs for the defenders as entire
formations and plans may be destroyed by the inside
information they possess. This group not only includes
informants and spies, but also covers collaborators from
within the government.

If a person is proven to be amongst this category, then
he/she may be fought and killed, or crucified and made as
a public example, or made disabled by the cutting off of
an alternate hand and foot, or banished permanently from
the land… However, if a traitor/spy/collaborator surrenders
and repents before being captured or discovered, then they
may be spared.

Logistical Support (Truck Drivers, Contractors, Cooks, etc.)

"When you were on the near side, and they were
on the far side, then the supply line became directly
beneath you. And if you had planned for this meeting,
you would have disagreed on its timing, but God was
to enforce a command that was already done. So that
He would destroy those to be destroyed with proof,
and to let those who will live be alive with proof; and
God is Hearer, Knowledgeable." (Qur'an 8:42)

Again, these are an "extension" of the invading army
and fall under the same ruling that it does. Without
the logistics of food, fuel, ammunition, clothes, etc. the

invading army would not have the ability to fight and to hold its positions. Attacking and destroying supply lines and logistic support is not only permissible, but is a requirement to put an end to the invading forces.

External Military Operations

"And why do you not fight in the cause of God, when the weak among the men and women and children say: 'Our Lord, bring us out of this town whose people are wicked, and grant us from Yourself a supporter, and grant us from Yourself a victor!'" (Qur'an 4:75)

"Those who have believed and emigrated and strived with their money and lives in the cause of God, and those who have sheltered and supported; these are the allies of one another. And those who believed but did not emigrate, you do not owe them any obligation until they emigrate. But if they seek your help in the system, then you must support them, except if it is against a people with whom there is a covenant between you and them. And God is Seer over what you do." (Qur'an 8:72)

"And if they break their oaths after making their pledge, and they challenge the authority of your system; then you may kill the leaders of rejection. Their oaths are nothing to them, perhaps they will then cease." (Qur'an 9:12)

"O you who believe, if you go forth in the cause of God, you shall investigate carefully. And do not say to those who greet you with peace: "You are not a believer!" You are seeking the vanity of this world; but with God are many riches. That is how you were before, but

God graced you, so investigate carefully. God is expert over what you do." (Qur'an 4:94)

Military action (outside the state or its boundaries) is only permitted under any of the following justifications:

- Coming to set free or relocate an oppressed people who have made a public call for help (in looking to the example of Moses and Pharaoh, there was no attempt made by Moses to change the government of Pharaoh or to give the Children of Israel power over the government or even to give them any part of the land of Egypt; he merely came to set them free and allow them to relocate and leave Egypt).

- A credible threat or action of threat is displayed by a group/nation against the Islamic state.

- In peacekeeping missions with nations/people with whom the state has a treaty.

The party being aggressed against must be formally and publicly made aware of the reasons for the attack and a reasonable opportunity be given to the nation which is about to be attacked to respond and amend.

Battle Strategy

This section is dedicated to the sharing of certain battle strategies and tips that have been ascertained from the Scripture:

Keep Organization and Planning Low Key

"And remember when you were but a few who were weak in the land, you were fearful that the people might capture you. But He sheltered you, and He supported you with His victory, and He provided you with good provisions, so that you may be thankful." (Qur'an 8:26)

Develop Weapons and Secure Funding

"And prepare for them all that you can of might, and from the steeds of war, that you may instill terror with it towards the enemy of God and your enemy, and others besides them whom you do not know but God knows them. And whatever you spend in the cause of God will be returned to you, and you will not be wronged." (Qur'an 8:60)

Research and Development

"That you may make armor coats that fit perfectly, and work righteousness. For I am Seer of what you do." (Qur'an 34:11)

"And We taught him the making of armor for you to protect you from your enemy. Are you then thankful?" (Qur'an 21:80)

Reconnaissance and Information Gathering

"But the hoopoe did not stay away long, then he said: 'I have seen what you do not know, and I have come to you from Sheba with news which is certain.'" (Qur'an 27:22)

Have Leadership in Place

"O you who believe, obey God and obey the messenger, and those in authority among you. But if you dispute in any matter, then you shall refer it to God and His messenger if you believe in God and the Last Day. That is better and more suitable for knowing." (Qur'an 4:59)

Mobilize Troops

"O you who believe, what is wrong with you when you are told: 'Mobilize in the cause of God,' you become heavy on the earth. Have you become content with this worldly life over the Hereafter? The enjoyment of this worldly life compared to the Hereafter is nothing." (Qur'an 9:38)

"Mobilize in light gear or heavy gear, and strive with your money and lives in the cause of God. That is best if only you knew." (Qur'an 9:41)

Attack Supply Lines

"When you were on the near side, and they were on the far side, then the supply line became directly beneath you. And if you had planned for this meeting, you would have disagreed on its timing, but God was to enforce a command that was already done. So that He would destroy those to be destroyed with proof, and to let those who will live be alive with proof; and God is Hearer, Knowledgeable." (Qur'an 8:42)

Coordinate Attacks

"God loves those who fight in His cause as one column; they are like bricks in a wall." (Qur'an 61:4)

Strike the Enemy Leadership

"And if they break their oaths after making their pledge, and they challenge the authority of your system; then you may kill the leaders of rejection.

Their oaths are nothing to them, perhaps they will then cease." (Qur'an 9:12)

Strike Weakest Links

"Therefore, if you encounter those who have rejected, then strike the necks; until you bind them, then secure the cords. You may then either set them free or ransom them, until the war ends. That, and if God had willed, He alone could have beaten them, but He thus tests you by one another. As for those who get killed in the cause of God, He will never let their deeds be put to waste." (Qur'an 47:4)

Follow Orders

"O you who believe, obey God and obey the messenger, and those in authority among you. But if you dispute in any matter, then you shall refer it to God and His messenger if you believe in God and the Last Day. That is better and more suitable for knowing." (Qur'an 4:59)

Scout Battle Terrain and Positions

"Remember when you departed from your family to prepare for the believers their stations for battle, and God is Hearer, Knowledgeable." (Qur'an 3:121)

Number of Fighters Irrelevant to Outcome

"God had granted you victory at Badr, while you had been the lesser, so reverence God that you may be thankful. When you said to the believers: 'Is it not enough for you that your Lord would supply

*you with three thousand of the angels sent down?
Indeed, if you are patient and are righteous and
they come and attack you, He will supply you
with five thousand of the angels battle trained.'"
(Qur'an 3:123-125)*

Hold Your Ground

*"O you who believe; when you encounter those who
have rejected on the battlefield, do not flee from them.
And whoever on that day flees from them; unless it is
part of the battle strategy or if he is retreating back to
his group; then he has drawn the wrath of God upon
him, and his abode will be Hell. What a miserable
destiny." (Qur'an 8:15-16)*

*"O you who believe, when you meet a force, stand firm
and mention God excessively, that you may succeed."
(Qur'an 8:45)*

Attack Bases of Traitors and Collaborators

*"And if you are being betrayed by a people, then you
shall likewise move against them. God does not love
the betrayers." (Qur'an 8:58)*

Encourage Populace to Fight or Defend

*"O prophet, urge the believers to fight. If there are
twenty of you who are patient, they will defeat two
hundred. And if there are one hundred of you, they
will defeat one thousand from among those who
reject; that is because they are a people who do not
understand." (Qur'an 8:65)*

Focus on Enemy Losses

"If you are wounded, then know that the other group is also wounded. And such are the days, We alternate them between the people, so that God will distinguish those who believe, and so He may make witnesses from among you; and God does not love the wicked." (Qur'an 3:140)

Change Plans That Do Not Work

"And so it was when you suffered setback; even though you afflicted them with twice as much setback; you said: 'Where is this coming from?' Say: 'It is from yourselves.' God is capable of all things." (Qur'an 3:165)

Replace Leadership If Killed or Captured, Focus on Final Goal

"And Mohammed is but a messenger, like many messengers who have passed before him. If he dies or is killed will you turn back on your heels? And whoever turns back on his heels, he will not harm God in the least. And God will recompense the thankful." (Qur'an 3:144)

Remember the Hereafter

"And if you are killed in the cause of God or die, then forgiveness from God and mercy are far greater than all they can put together. And if you die or are killed, then to God you will be gathered. And do not think that those who are killed in the cause of God are dead. No, they are alive at their Lord receiving a bounty. Happy with what God has granted them from His grace, and they rejoice in those who have yet to follow

after them. There is no fear upon them nor do they grieve. They rejoice with the bounty of God and grace; God will not waste the recompense of the believers." (Qur'an 3:169–171)

Trust in God

"The ones who the people said to them: 'The people have gathered against you, so be concerned by them,' but it only increased their faith and they said: 'God is sufficient for us, and He is the best to put our trust in.'" (Qur'an 3:173)

"And when the believers saw the opponents, they said: 'This is what God and His messenger have promised us, and God and His messenger are truthful.' This only increased their faith and their submission." (Qur'an 33:22)

Scope of Warfare and Conduct

"And if they cease, then God is Forgiving, Merciful. And fight them so there is no more persecution, and so that the system is for God. If they cease, then there will be no aggression except against the wicked." (Qur'an 2:192–193)

With the exception of defensive warfare which is conducted until the enemy/invader is completely driven out or surrenders, all other warfare conducted by the state is to be done while exercising patience and restraint at all times. The combat personnel are prohibited from fighting or attacking non-combatants in any shape, way or form, unless they have placed themselves within the territory of the state and are being driven out (i.e. settlers that have come with the invading army) or have become intermingled with the invading army. Combatants who withdraw to territories of nations with which the state has a covenant/treaty may not be harmed as long as they are not launching attacks from such territory.

Prisoners of War

> "And it was not for any prophet to take prisoners until he is bound by a campaign. You desire the materials of this world, while God wants the Hereafter for you. God is Noble, Wise." (Qur'an 8:67)

> "O prophet, say to those prisoners whom you hold: 'If God finds in your hearts any good, He will grant you better than what He took from you, and He will forgive you. God is Forgiving, Merciful.'" (Qur'an 8:70)

> "Therefore, if you encounter those who have rejected, then strike the necks; until you bind them, then secure the cords. You may then either set them free or ransom them, until the war ends. That, and if God had willed, He alone could have beaten them, but He thus tests you by one another. As for those who get killed in the cause of God, He will never let their deeds be put to waste." (Qur'an 47:4)

Prisoners are only taken in battle or warfare and not during peacetime or non-combative action.

Prisoners of war are to be treated with dignity and respect at all times and must be provided food, shelter and medical assistance. Prisoners are not to be humiliated, tortured or subjected to psychological or physical stress at any time during their captivity.

Prisoners may be exchanged or set free during a war based on what is deemed to be in the best interest of the state. However, once the war is officially over, then all prisoners must be released immediately and returned to their homeland or given shelter in the state if that is their request and it is deemed to represent no threat.

Desertion

"O you who believe; when you encounter those who have rejected on the battlefield, do not flee from them. And whoever on that day flees from them; unless it is part of the battle strategy or if he is retreating back to his group; then he has drawn the wrath of God upon him, and his abode will be Hell. What a miserable destiny." (Qur'an 8:15-16)

Desertion from the military or from battle shall inflict action against the offending person through the criminal court of the state.

The Ending of Military Conflict

"And fight in the cause of God against those who fight you, but do not aggress, God does not love the aggressors. And kill them wherever you overcome them, and expel them from where they expelled you, and know that persecution is worse than being killed. And do not fight them at the Restricted Temple unless they fight you in it; if they fight you then kill them, thus is the recompense of the disbelievers." (Qur'an 2:190-191)

"And if they seek peace, then you also seek it, and put your trust in God. He is the Hearer, the Knowledgeable. And if they wish to deceive you, then God is sufficient for you. He is the One who supported you with His victory and with the believers." (Qur'an 8:61-62)

The military campaign can only end with the invaders being driven out (if it is a defensive war) or if the state decides to cease the military campaign (if it is an aggressive war). No treaties or withdrawals are permitted in a defensive war until the enemy has fully withdrawn from all occupied areas or has surrendered. If the enemy has withdrawn, then a peace treaty may be held if the aggressor requests it.

Spoils of War

> "They ask you regarding the spoils of war, say: 'The spoils of war are for God and the messenger.' So be aware of God, and be upright in matters between you; and obey God and His messenger if you are believers." (Qur'an 8:1)

In war, all spoils are to be administered by the state for distribution into the economy and people.

Secret Operations/Missions

> "They ask you regarding the crescent moons, say: 'They are a timing mechanism for the people and the Pilgrimage.' And piety is not that you would enter a home from its back, but piety is whoever is righteous and comes to the homes from their main doors. And be aware of God that you may succeed." (Qur'an 2:189)

The Islamic state and all its citizens are *prohibited* from conducting secret warfare or operations designed to destabilize, undermine or corrupt the systems of foreign nations. The state will always be bound by transparency and honesty and the desire to benefit the lives of humans inside the state and elsewhere on Earth.

Campaigns of Conquest

> *"If you sought conquest, then conquest has come to you, but if you cease, then it is better for you. And if you return again, then We will also return, and your group will avail you nothing even if it is many. God is with the believers." (Qur'an 8:19)*

Campaigns with the intent of conquest are prohibited from being conducted.

Peace Keeping Efforts

> *"And if two parties of believers battle with each other, you shall reconcile them; but if one of them aggresses against the other, then you shall fight the one aggressing until it complies with the command of God. Once it complies, then you shall reconcile the two groups with justice, and be equitable; for God loves those who are equitable. The believers are brothers; so reconcile between your brothers, and be aware of God, that you may receive mercy." (Qur'an 49:9–10)*

The Scripture allows for the state to enter into peacekeeping missions. Such missions shall be limited to ending the aggression of one party against another and reconciliation between the two warring factions.

13

The Calendar System

Creating a vibrant republic based on the Scripture does not only rely on laws and legal issues but must also take into account the advanced requirement of "time keeping."

Below is a brief history of some of the most widely used calendars that may assist us in understanding how the celestial system of God has been put in use over the ages.

Egyptian Calendar
It is recorded that the early Egyptians (around 4,000 BC) used a Solar calendar of 365 days based on their

observation of the star Sirius rising with the Sun (this is the Heliacal rising and would occur at the peak of summer). The Egyptians also had 12 months in their year divided into 30 days each. The last 5 days were called "days of festival" (20:59) and were not part of any month.

They eventually had a system of 36 stars to mark out the year and in the end had three different calendars working concurrently for over 2000 years: a stellar calendar for agriculture, a solar year of 365 days (12 months x 30 + 5 extra) for civil life, and a quasi-lunar calendar for festivals. The later Egyptian calendars developed sophisticated Zodiac systems.

Greek Calendar

The calendar used by the ancient Greeks was based on the Moon and was known as the Metonic calendar. This calendar was based on the observations of Meton of Athens (ca. 440 BC), which showed that 235 lunar months made up almost exactly 19 solar years. This 19-year cycle became known as the Metonic cycle. However, given a nominal twelve-month year, an additional lunar month needed to be added to synchronize the cycle. These were added in years 3, 5, 8, 11, 13, 16, and 19 of the cycle.

Thus the Greek Calendar is a mixture of Solar and Lunar elements.

Roman Calendar

The Romans started off with a 10 month Lunar calendar which started the year around the vernal equinox and consisted of 10 months (Martius, Aprilis, Maius, Junius, Quntilis, Sextilis, September, October, November, and December) having a total of 304 days. The 304 days were followed by an unnamed, unnumbered period in winter. The Roman emperor Numa Pompilius (715-673 BC) introduced February and January between December and March, increasing the length of the year to 354 or 355 days.

In 46 BC, the Romans altered their calendar based on the Egyptian model, under emperor Julius Caesar, to a calendar made up of 365 days (366 in a leap-year). Also, the number of days per month was altered/increased to correspond to the 365-day year (i.e. 31 day months were introduced).

Gregorian Calendar

This is the most common calendar in use today in the modern world and is an adjustment of the earlier Roman Calendar. Julian Scaliger defined Day One (January 1st) as a day when three cycles converged on it. The first cycle was the 28 year period over which the Julian calendar repeats. The second was the 19 year golden number cycle over which phases of the moon almost land on the same dates of the year. The third cycle was the 15 year ancient Roman tax cycle of emperor Constantine.

In 1582 Pope Gregory truncated 10 days off the Roman calendar to bring it in line with the vernal equinox (errors were previously made in the leap-year adjustments and the calendar slipped out of sync with the seasons).

Jewish Calendar

The Hebrew calendar is a blend of Lunar and Solar components resulting in what is called a "Luni-Solar" calendar. The religious beginning of the Hebrew calendar is the month of Nisan (based on Exodus 12:2) which corresponds to the months of March or April depending on the lunar and solar cycles.

The Hebrew months are: (Tishri, Heshvan, Kislev, Tevet, Shevat, Adar, Nisan, Iyar, Sivan, Tammuz, Av, Elul). The extra month (called Adar II) is inserted roughly every 7 years to make-up for the 11-day slip which results from following the Lunar cycles. This adjustment is done to keep the calendar in line with the seasons of a Solar year.

Current Islamic Calendar

The current Islamic calendar uses a simple count of 12 lunar months, which presumes to be based on the Scripture and uses the Hijra (the migration of the Prophet to Medina) as its "year zero."

> "The count of the months with God is twelve months in the book of God the day He created the heavens and the earth; four of them are restricted. This is the correct system; so do not wrong yourselves in them; and fight the polytheists collectively as they fight you collectively. And know that God is with the righteous." (Qur'an 9:36)

The lunar months retain Arabic names in the following sequence:

1. Muharam,
2. Safar,
3. Rabea I,
4. Rabea II,
5. Jamadi I,
6. Jamadi II,
7. Rajab,
8. Shaban,
9. Ramadhan,
10. Shawal,
11. Dhul Qida,
12. Dhul Hija.

The obvious result of such a calendar, as any amateur astronomer would know, is that the lunar year (12 months x 29.53 days per month = 354.36 days) will be 11 days shorter than the actual solar year of 365.242 days. This calendar results in the months being wildly out of sync with the seasons, and any future planning becomes a complexity in itself.

It is no secret that nearly all nations who profess to use the Islamic calendar will also run a civil calendar that uses a 365-day year and for which they schedule their lives and businesses.

Definition of a Year

The first question that needs to be asked when constructing any calendar is whether to use a solar year of 365 days (representing the length of time it takes the Earth to rotate completely around the sun), or, whether to use a lunar year by simply counting 12 lunar months (354 days), or, whether to use a mixture of both solar and lunar at the same time.

> "And We made the night and the day as two signs, so We erased the sign of night and We made the sign of day to see-in, that you may seek bounty from your Lord, and that you may know the number of the years and the count. And everything We have detailed completely." (Qur'an 17:12)

> "He is the One who has made the sun a radiance, and the moon a light, and He has measured its phases; that you may know the number of the years and the count. God has not created this except with the truth. He clarifies the revelations for a people who know." (Qur'an 10:5)

According to the above verses, the main theme that is used to measure the year is the alternation of the day and night (which is caused by the movement of the Earth around the sun), while the secondary theme are the phases of the moon, thus making the calendar that is described in the Scripture of God as being "luni-solar" in nature.

Year = 365 days rounded (365.24 days—one full rotation around the sun)

We can see this reference to a solar based 365-day year in the story of Joseph when he refers to the seven years of drought that Egypt will face (12:47) as it is linked directly to the harvest, as well as the unique phenomenon that the singular word 'day/yawm' occurs in the entire Qur'an an exact 365 times.

Definition of a Month

With regards to a 'month,' it is a unit of measure that is contained within a year (established as 365 days). According to the Scripture, there are 12 of these units 'months' that are counted within the system of the year:

> *"The count of the months with God is twelve months in the book of God the day He created the heavens and the earth; four of them are restricted. This is the correct system; so do not wrong yourselves in them; and fight the polytheists collectively as they fight you collectively. And know that God is with the righteous." (Qur'an 9:36)*

Therefore, and in the simplest terms, the average length of each month is $365 \div 12 = 30.4$ days (30 days rounded).

This figure of 30 days brings us back to the moon whereby we are told that, in addition to the sun, the moon is also related to the count of the years.

> *"He is the One who has made the sun a radiance, and the moon a light, and He has measured its phases; that you may know the number of the years and the count. God has not created this except with the truth. He clarifies the revelations for a people who know." (Qur'an 10:5)*

The average length of the cycle of the moon is 29.53 days (30 days rounded), which is in-line with the measure of the '30-day month' as given in the Scripture.

Month = 30 days rounded (29.53 days —one full lunar cycle)

We can see the correlation between thirty days and one month clearly in verse 58:4 which speaks of a person fasting for "two consecutive months" or "feeding sixty poor" thus making the definition of a month as 30 days.

When does the year begin?

The current dates used in modern calendars to mark the first day of the year (such as January 1st in the Gregorian calendar or Muharam in the Arabic calendar) are arbitrary dates that have been selected based on specific historic events (the death of Jesus in the Gregorian, and the Hijra of the Prophet in the Arabic).

According to the Qur'an, the most significant event that takes place on one night every year is the "Night of Decree" in which the angels and the Spirit are sent down to carry out the decrees of God:

> *"We have sent it down in the Night of Decree. And do you know what is the Night of Decree? The Night of Decree is better than one thousand months. The angels and the Spirit come down in it with the permission of their Lord to carry out every matter. It is peaceful until the coming of dawn." (Qur'an 97:1-5)*

This event, being a blessed night for the receipt of the commands of God, is by far the most significant and the most worthy to be used as a marker for the beginning of the year.

Jesus and the Night of Decree

The birth of the Messiah, Jesus, is amongst the greatest miracles to occur in our history as he was conceived miraculously without having a father and he was able to speak to people from the cradle and was able to perform great miracles (with the permission of God) that included raising the dead and healing the blind and the lepers.

Accordingly, the Qur'an gives us some clues regarding this great event, specifically in identifying the period/ month in which the son of Mary was given birth to:

"And shake the trunk of this palm tree, it will cause ripe dates (Rutab) *to fall upon you." (Qur'an 19:25)*

The term "Rutab" indicates an advanced level of date ripening. The known time for this stage of date development typically occurs in the Middle East at the end of the peak of hot season and dates are known as "Rutab" from the period ending in August till the period ending in September.

As such, it is with this clue that we can determine that the Messiah was given birth to in the period around September according to the climate of the Middle East.

However, it is not in the birth of Jesus that we find clues to the Night of Decree, rather, it is with the night of his conception.

"So she took a barrier to separate her from them, so We sent Our Spirit to her, and he took on the shape of a man in all similarity. She said: 'I seek refuge with the Almighty from you if you are righteous.' He said: 'I am the messenger of your Lord, to grant you the gift of a pure son.'" (Qur'an 19:17-19)

"And the angels said: 'O Mary, God gives you glad tidings of a word from Him. His name is the Messiah, Jesus the son of Mary. Honorable in this world and in the Hereafter, and from among those who are made close. And he will speak to the people from the cradle and to middle-age, and is from among the upright.' She said: 'My Lord, how can I have a son when no man has been with me?' He said: 'It is thus that God creates what He wills, when He decrees a command, He merely says to it 'Be,' and it is.'" (Qur'an 3:45-47)

The Spirits and the Angels Come Down

The Night of Decree is unique in that the Angels and the Spirit are said to come down to carry out the commands of the Lord:

"The angels and the Spirit come down in it with the permission of their Lord to carry out every matter." (Qur'an 97:4)

With regards to Jesus, this event took place on the eve of his conception, thus making the Night of Decree occur 9 months prior to his birth (i.e. around December).

Night of Decree = Spirit + Angels
Conception of Jesus = Spirit + Angels
Night of Decree = On or about December

Now that the evidence has been presented to gauge the

period of the Night of Decree, it is only reasonable to pursue the subject further and try to ascertain "which night."

Throughout the Qur'an we are told that God favors the night for worship and for His messages:

- The Qur'an was sent at night (44:3, 97:1);

- God commanded Moses to wait for 40 nights (7:142);

- Worship is spoken of as occurring during the night (39:9, 73:20);

- Salat occurs with the beginning of night as well as its end (24:58);

- God took the Prophet on a special journey at night (17:1);

- The Qur'an is best studied at night (17:79);

- Zakariya was commanded to fast from speaking for three nights (19:10).

Since the night is more precious than the day, then it is only normal that we look at the days with the "longest" nights as being possible candidates since we know that God in His mercy would want to give humankind the maximum benefit of His blessings and not anything lesser:

> "Say: 'If you were the ones possessing the vaults of the mercy of my Lord, you would have held back for concern of spending. And the human being was always stingy!'" (Qur'an 17:100)

Interestingly enough, a little research reveals that there is indeed one day every year which, according to astronomy, is unique in being the day with the *longest night*. More interestingly, we find that this day occurs in none other than the month of December of each year.

The Winter Solstice, also known as Midwinter, occurs around December 21 or 22 each year in the Northern hemisphere. It occurs on the longest night of the year, sometimes said to mark the beginning of an astronomical winter for a hemisphere.

http://en.wikipedia.org/wiki/Winter_solstice

Night of Decree = December 21st or 22nd each year

Now that we have a marker to begin the year with, it is time to look at the other elements that together make a working calendar based on the Qur'an.

The Lunar Month

Since we are told that the count of the year not only involves the 'sun' but the 'moon' also, then we need to determine which phase of the moon (dark moon, to crescent, to full moon, to crescent, to dark moon) signifies the beginning of any given month.

> *"They ask you regarding the crescent moons, say: 'They are a timing mechanism for the people and the Pilgrimage.' And piety is not that you would*

165

enter a home from its back, but piety is whoever is righteous and comes to the homes from their main doors. And be aware of God that you may succeed." (Qur'an 2:189)

From reading the verse above, we can conclude that the crescent moon did not signify the start of the lunar cycle as the question signifies the people were unsure where to place such a phase (yet the count of the months was already well established and well known as evidenced by 9:37) and the answer they were given linked the crescent mainly to the start of the Pilgrimage period.

We are now left with two options for the beginning of the month:

- Dark moon
- Full moon

"And the moon We have measured it to appear in stages, until it returns like an old curved sheath." (Qur'an 36:39)

The 'old curved sheath' of a palm tree is the section of branch that dies and then hangs down in a curved shape on either side of the tree.

The only time we can see this phenomenon with the moon is during a 'full moon' when the darkness of the night sky makes a curved shape on the left and on the right (like an old curved sheath which has died and changed its color from the original tree).

Therefore, the months begin with the full moon.

The Four Restricted Months
The other piece of information we are given to incorporate into a calendar are the 'four restricted months' in which hunting of all wild game is forbidden (with the exception of any catch from the sea).

> "The count of the months with God is twelve months in the book of God the day He created the heavens and the earth; four of them are restricted. This is the correct system; so do not wrong yourselves in them; and fight the polytheists collectively as they fight you collectively. And know that God is with the righteous." (Qur'an 9:36)

> "O you who believe, honor your contracts. Made lawful for you are all the animals of the livestock, except that which is being recited to you. You are not permitted to

hunt the game while you are under restriction. God decrees as He pleases." (Qur'an 5:1)

"Lawful for you is the catch of the sea, to eat it as enjoyment for you and for those who travel; and unlawful for you is the catch of the land as long as you are under restriction; and be aware of God to whom you will be gathered." (Qur'an 5:96)

Further study reveals that these four months occur during the winter/spring season(s) as evidenced by a four month ultimatum being issued during the greater Pilgrimage which expired with the onset of the summer heat:

"Therefore, roam the land for four months and know that you will not escape God, and that God will humiliate the rejecters. And a declaration from God and His messenger to the people on the day of the greater Pilgrimage: "That God and His messenger are innocent from the polytheists." If you repent, then it is better for you, and if you turn away, then know that you will not escape God. And give news to those who have rejected of a painful retribution. Except for those with whom you had made a pledge from among the polytheists if they did not reduce anything from it nor did they plan to attack you; you shall continue the pledge with them until its expiry. God loves the righteous. So when the restricted months have passed, then you may kill the polytheists wherever you find them, and take them, and surround them, and stand against them at every point. If they repent, and they hold the contact prayer, and they contribute towards purification, then you shall leave them alone. God is Forgiving, Merciful." (Qur'an 9:2-5)

*"Those who have remained are happy with their
position of lagging behind the messenger of God, and
they disliked striving with their money and lives in
the cause of God; and they say: 'Do not mobilize in
the heat.' Say: 'The fire of Hell is much hotter,' if they
could only understand." (Qur'an 9:81)*

What we can establish further is that the Pilgrimage
is held for at least three months (plural use of the word
"months" indicated three or more 2:197). Also we can
establish that one of the four restricted months is 'special'
in that it is referred to on several occasions on its own
(2:217, 5:2, 5:97). Finally, we can determine that the
"special" month is none other than the month of fasting
"Ramadhan" which is the only month referred to on its
own, and which happens to be the month in which the
Qur'an was revealed—taking us back to the special Night
of Decree.

Night of Decree = Month of Ramadhan = One of the
Restricted Months

Returning to the ultimatum given in 9:2-5, we find that
this four month ultimatum was given during the "greater
Pilgrimage" which makes it the last in the sequences of
the pilgrimage months (the first linguistically being the
"smaller," the second being the "great," and the final being
the "greater") and as we know that this ultimatum ended
with the advent of the summer heat, thus the sequence we
find is as follows:

Restricted Month-1 = Ramadhan

(includes the Night of Decree)

Restricted Month-2 = Smaller Pilgrimage

Restricted Month-3 = Great Pilgrimage

Restricted Month-4 = Greater Pilgrimage

The 13th month?

While having a luni-solar year is extremely accurate when it comes to aligning the year with the seasons, planning for crops and harvests, and in knowing the natural cycle of wildlife, there is one issue that needs to be addressed which is the '13th month' (intercalary month) that occurs in some solar years due to the length of a lunar month being on average 29.54 days and thus not fitting perfectly in a 365 day year.

The Scripture tells us that previous generations manipulated the thirteenth month by inserting it in one year and removing it from the next so as to circumvent the hunting restrictions placed by God:

> *"Know that the use of the additional month causes an increase in rejection, for it is used by those who have rejected that they may misguide with it by making it lawful one year, and unlawful one year, so as to circumvent the count of what God has made restricted; thus they make lawful what God has made unlawful. Their evil works have been adorned for them, and God does not guide the rejecting people." (Qur'an 9:37)*

The correct approach with regards to the intercalary month is to apply it at the end of the year where, after the count of twelve months/moons, the new full moon would fall 30-days short of the Night of Decree.

Such application gives us a total of seven intercalary months inserted in every nineteen year cycle.

Conclusion

The calendar of God is one that exists in nature and which utilizes the entities of sun, moon and star to make a perfect timing mechanism that is in-line with nature and in-harmony with our movements through the universe.

Summary:

- The year according to the Scripture is 365 days (12:47, 17:12);

- The calendar system for the year is luni-solar (17:12, 10:5);

- The most special event that occurs during the year is the Night of Decree (97:4) which occurs on the winter solstice.

- The count of the months begins with the full moon (2:189, 36:39).

- The month of the winter solstice is known as the month of "Ramadhan" (2:185).

- The month of Ramadhan is 'Month-1' in the Islamic calendar;

- Three months of Pilgrimage follow the month of Ramadhan—all four months are restricted from hunting any game, while domestic animals and the catch of the sea are lawful (9:2-5, 2:217, 5:1, 5:96);

- After a count of 12 lunar months, if a 13th full moon appears a full 30 days before the next winter solstice, then such a month is to be ignored and counted as 'month zero'.

Sample Calendar (2008-2012)

Gregorian Date	Corrected Muslim Calendar	Type of Month
November 24th, 2007	1st Month	Restricted
December 24th, 2007	2nd Month	Restricted
January 22nd, 2008	3rd Month	Restricted
February 21st, 2008	4th Month	Restricted
March 21st, 2008	5th Month	Normal
April 20th, 2008	6th Month	Normal

May 20th, 2008	7th Month	Normal
June 18th, 2008	8th Month	Normal
July 18th, 2008	9th Month	Normal
August 16th, 2008	10th Month	Normal
September 15th, 2008	11th Month	Normal
October 14th, 2008	12th Month	Normal
November 13th, 2008	13th Month	Normal
December 12th, 2008	1st Month	Restricted
January 11th, 2009	2nd Month	Restricted
February 9th, 2009	3rd Month	Restricted
March 11th, 2009	4th Month	Restricted
April 9th, 2009	5th Month	Normal
May 9th, 2009	6th Month	Normal
June 7th, 2009	7th Month	Normal
July 7th, 2009	8th Month	Normal
August 6th, 2009	9th Month	Normal
September 4th, 2009	10th Month	Normal
October 4th, 2009	11th Month	Normal
November 2nd, 2009	12th Month	Normal
December 2nd, 2009	1st Month	Restricted
December 31st, 2009	2nd Month	Restricted
January 30th, 2010	3rd Month	Restricted
February 28th, 2010	4th Month	Restricted
March 30th, 2010	5th Month	Normal
April 28th, 2010	6th Month	Normal
May 27th, 2010	7th Month	Normal
June 26th, 2010	8th Month	Normal
July 26th, 2010	9th Month	Normal
August 24th, 2010	10th Month	Normal
September 23rd, 2010	11th Month	Normal
October 23rd, 2010	12th Month	Normal
November 21st, 2010	13th Month	Normal
December 21st, 2010	1st Month	Restricted
January 19th, 2011	2nd Month	Restricted

February 18th, 2011	3rd Month	Restricted
March 19th, 2011	4th Month	Restricted
April 18th, 2011	5th Month	Normal
May 17th, 2011	6th Month	Normal
June 15th, 2011	7th Month	Normal
July 15th, 2011	8th Month	Normal
August 13th, 2011	9th Month	Normal
September 12th, 2011	10th Month	Normal
October 12th, 2011	11th Month	Normal
November 10th, 2011	12th Month	Normal
December 10th, 2011	1st Month	Restricted
January 9th, 2012	2nd Month	Restricted
February 7th, 2012	3rd Month	Restricted
March 8th, 2012	4th Month	Restricted
April 6th, 2012	5th Month	Normal
May 6th, 2012	6th Month	Normal
June 4th, 2012	7th Month	Normal
July 3rd, 2012	8th Month	Normal
August 2nd, 2012	9th Month	Normal
August 31st, 2012	10th Month	Normal
September 30th, 2012	11th Month	Normal
October 29th, 2012	12th Month	Normal
November 28th, 2012	1st Month	Restricted
December 28th, 2012	2nd Month	Restricted

Future dates for the full moon may be obtained from the following source: http://aa.usno.navy.mil/data/docs/MoonPhase.html

14

A New Beginning

The historic progression Islam has gone through since the Scripture was delivered by the Prophet Mohammed with regards to government has been to move from a council type government formed under the Prophet (Shoura) to a myriad of different systems of governments with Kings, Sultans, Presidents, and Sheikhs appearing all across the former Islamic world.

While all these one-man dictators are still with us today, the masses are convinced that a return to the "Khilafa" (Supreme Islamic Leader) is the solution to their ills and dysfunctional governments. Of course, the Khilafa is nothing but a one-man government (one person with all powers vested in him), so they would not really be making much difference from where they are today!

When studying the Qur'an, we find two forms of government highlighted:

1. Kings appointed by God to rule with His laws (e.g. David, Solomon, Saul 38:17-20, 2:102, 2:247);

2. Model governments built on consultation (e.g. Sheba, Prophet Mohammed 27:32, 3:159).

A monarch appointed by God has not been in effect for many centuries and will therefore not be discussed for the purpose of this chapter, except to say that a monarchy established by men has been condemned in the Qur'an (27:34, 18:79, 43:51). However, a government built on consultation is given with live examples and it will be such that we use to base our foundation upon.

The structure of government within the Scripture gives way to a republic that has been designed to ensure protection of its citizens' rights as well as to create a vibrant and dynamic government to manage the needs and aspirations of its citizens. The structure is designed to create checks and balances whereby no one branch of government or one person may control the entire government.

This chapter will deal with the creation of such a government, to the point of having a written constitution available for implementation.

Proposed Constitution

The constitution proposed in this section, and which would be ready for implementation in any populated area or region, represents the core values and attributes of the Scripture in justice, equality, representation, transparency, and freedoms.

The Natural Republic Constitution

We, the people of [insert name of country/province], hereby decree our acceptance to the establishment of this constitution in order to promote justice, fairness, equality, freedom, and the pursuit of security and happiness for all.[6]

ARTICLE I

This constitution, and its subsequent laws, shall override and supersede any existing constitutions, treaties, agreements, legislations and/or laws.

This constitution shall take effect in all provinces and geographic areas currently known as [insert name of country/province] which has been defined by mutually agreed borders.

Citizens are deemed as those persons who legally carry the [insert name of country/province] nationality at the time of implementing this constitution.

All adult citizens of the republic are required to give an oath of allegiance to uphold and defend this constitution at all times .[7]

The Qur'an shall be the basis for this constitution and shall be the source for all the legislation and laws of the republic.[8]

[insert name of capital city] shall be designated as the permanent capital for the republic.

[insert language(s)] shall be the official language(s) of the republic.

ARTICLE II

The freedoms and rights granted in this article are available to every adult person in the republic, regardless of gender,

---

6 Qur'an 16:90-91

7 Qur'an 48:10

8 Qur'an 17:9, 5:48

race, nationality, color, or creed. Such freedoms and rights may not be suspended, diluted, or obstructed.

Freedom of Speech
All persons have the right of free speech, freedom of the media, the right to assemble, and the right to protest peacefully.[9]

Freedom of Faith
All persons have the right to believe in any faith or religion they may see fit. The freedom of faith includes the establishment of temples, mosques, synagogues, churches, and any other constructs used for such purpose.[10]

Freedom of Movement
All persons may travel freely throughout the public lands of the republic, exit and/or enter its borders, in a legal manner, with no hindrance or delay. Such right extends to include the movement of goods.[11]

Right to Privacy
All persons have the right to privacy against spying, eavesdropping, trespassing, entering homes without the permission of the owner, obtaining, and/or sharing private information.[12]

Right to Possess Wealth
All persons have the right to seek to possess wealth, and/or assets, and/or to engage in trade, industry, commerce and/or any other legally sanctioned activities.[13]

---

9 Qur'an 71:5-9

10 Qur'an 10:99, 18:29, 88:21-22

11 Qur'an 29:56

12 Qur'an 24:27-29, 49:12

13 Qur'an 3:14

Right to Welfare

All persons have the right to be granted security, education, and equal employment opportunities within the ability of the republic.[14]

Right against Discrimination

All persons are to be granted equal rights and opportunities irrespective of race, gender, color, faith, and any other discrimination.[15]

Right to Seek Justice

All persons and/or legal entities have the right to demand justice against any wrongdoing or crime that befalls them without obstruction or undue delay.[16]

ARTICLE III

The legislative powers of the republic shall be vested in an elected national council that shall be representative of the people and which shall conduct its business through the process of open discussion and consultation in all matters.[17]

Elections will be based on districts, whereby each district is defined as an independent area with a minimum citizen population of one percent of the total population of the republic.

Areas that have populations below one percent shall have their number added to the nearest geographic area until that number reaches or exceeds one percent. Seats for the national council will be allotted on the basis of a minimum of one seat for every district, with districts having populations in multiples of one percent being

---

14 Qur'an 30:38, 59:7

15 Qur'an 49:13

16 Qur'an 4:148, 42:39

17 Qur'an 42:38

allotted one extra seat for each multiple.

Persons eligible for the national council must be citizens, male or female, forty years of age or older, of sound mind and character and must be residents of the district they are elected from.[18]

Eligible voters shall be as those male and female citizens who have reached the age of eighteen or older, and who are present within the borders of the republic at the time of voting.

Seats to the national council will be granted to those nominees who achieve a majority vote from the district where they reside. Votes in single member districts will be made on the basis of alternative voting, while votes in multiple member districts will be made on the basis of single transferable voting.

National council members, unless re-elected, shall serve one term of five years beginning on the first day of the first month of the new year.

Elections shall be concluded 90-days prior to the end of the existing national council members' term of office to ensure a smooth transition and hand-over of duties and responsibilities.

In cases of death or resignation, a new national council member shall be elected from the same district to serve the remaining term of the departed national council member.

Each national council member carries one vote with the council decisions becoming law based on a two thirds (2/3) or more vote on the issue(s).

The national council is granted the following powers:

- The power to make, review, amend, and repeal laws in accordance with the principles of justice.[19]

- The power to make policies and strategies necessary to ensure the smooth functioning of

18 Qur'an 46:15, 49:13

19 Qur'an 4:58

the republic.[20]

- The power to appoint and/or renew a president and his/her ministers for a term totaling five years.[21]

- The power to prematurely end the term of the president or any of his/her ministers.[22]

- The power to regulate new citizenship requirements.[23]

- The power to appropriate payment and compensation schemes for all levels of government, including the national council.[24]

- The power to stipulate taxation for individuals and corporations, on condition that such taxation does not exceed 20 percent.[25]

- The power to establish the benchmark for weights, measures, time keeping, and minimum wages within the republic.[26]

- The power to coin money as legal tender, only if such money is coined in gold or silver or backed by gold or silver.[27]

- The power to lend and/or borrow money, interest free, on behalf of the republic.[28]

- The power to lease public lands for the purpose

20 Qur'an 12:47-49

21 Qur'an 4:59

22 Qur'an 58:11

23 Qur'an 60:10

24 Qur'an 28:27

25 Qur'an 8:41

26 Qur'an 6:152, 7:85

27 Qur'an 9:34

28 Qur'an 2:275, 2:282

of development and betterment.[29]

- The power to preserve and protect wildlife and the natural ecological balance.[30]

- The power to allocate funds and approve budgets for all government agencies.[31]

- The power to call for audits on any branch/department/agency of government.[32]

- The power to initiate, locally and/or abroad, legal proceedings and/or claims on behalf of the republic.[33]

- The power to enter into treaties and/or agreements with foreign nations/peoples.[34]

- The power to establish a military for land, sea, and air.[35]

- The power to establish a security force for the protection of people and their rights within the republic.[36]

- The power to mediate, through peaceful means, an end to armed conflict in/or between foreign nations.[37]

- The power to aid and/or assist oppressed people in foreign nations, by granting them asylum and/or negotiating on their behalf, on condition

29 Qur'an 7:74
30 Qur'an 5:1-2, 30:41
31 Qur'an 17:27-29
32 Qur'an 17:36
33 Qur'an 42:39
34 Qur'an 8:72
35 Qur'an 8:60
36 Qur'an 22:41
37 Qur'an 49:9-10

that they have requested such help.[38]

- The power to provide humanitarian aid and/or assistance for crisis relief of any foreign nation and/or people in need.[39]

- The power to declare war and appropriate a war cabinet if the republic is under physical attack, and/or economic attack, and/or if its security and/or citizens are under an imminent and recognizable threat of attack.[40]

- The power to call for a public draft in defense of the republic and its lands if the republic is attacked or under an imminent and recognizable threat of attack.[41]

The national council shall elect a speaker from amongst the national council members to regulate the proceedings of its assemblies.

The national council shall assemble, at a minimum, every ninety days, for a length of three days to discuss legislation and/or appropriation and/or any matters that concern the well being of the republic and its citizens. The national council may vote to shorten or extend the length of such assembly based on requirements.

The national council may also be called for assembly at any other time during the year at the request, submitted to the speaker, of at least one third of the total national council members. Such announcement for assembly must be broadcast publicly and clearly, as well as the requirements that the request be made in writing to all national council members.

---

38 Qur'an 4:75, 8:72

39 Qur'an 2:177

40 Qur'an 2:190-193

41 Qur'an 8:65, 9:41

During times of war and/or danger, the national council may be excluded from physical assembly and decisions may be conducted by way of obtaining signatures from the respective council members to meet the two-third or more required votes.

ARTICLE IV

The executive powers of the republic shall be vested in a president who shall be appointed by the national council.[42]

The president shall be responsible for the selection of his/her cabinet of ministers to be presented for approval by the national council.

The president shall be responsible for carrying out the approved policies and strategies of the national council.

The president shall be responsible for the administration and management of all branches of government in the republic, setting rules and regulations necessary to ensure the smooth functioning of such branches, and budget preparation.

The president shall be responsible for the planning, budgeting, and execution of all public projects including: factories, farms, roads, power, exploration, mining, drilling, refinement, water treatment, transportation, mail delivery, sewage treatment, public offices/buildings, libraries, schools, hospitals, social services, and any other construct or activity required for the service of the public or the betterment of life for people under the republic.

The president shall be responsible for the regulation of all private sector activities/projects including: manufacturing, mining, energy, agriculture, trade, services, construction, transport, travel, education, medical, technology, charities, and any other activity or construct that is requested by people in the republic.

The president shall represent the republic before foreign

---

42 Qur'an 27:32

dignitaries/nations and may engage in negotiations/ discussions, which are not binding except with the ratification of the national council, regarding all matters that concern the republic.

The president shall present a detailed report of his/ her activities prior to every scheduled national council assembly. The president will also make himself/herself present at the scheduled national council assembly or at the request of the council speaker for non-scheduled sessions in order to give a briefing on the state of the republic as well as answering any questions/clarifications required by the council members.

ARTICLE V

The judicial powers of the republic shall be vested in an independent high court and its subsequent lower courts that shall judge according to the laws as placed by the national council.[43]

The high court shall comprise of twelve justices who shall be appointed by the national council and who shall hold office as long as they maintain integrity, proper conduct, and adherence to the laws of the constitution.

The high court shall have the responsibility of appointing court judges, presiding over cases of treason, and presiding over legal proceedings and/or impeachment charges made against the president, cabinet ministers, and/or any national council member(s).

The high court will also have the final say in appeal matters over lower courts.

The decisions of the high court are binding based on a two-thirds or more vote.[44]

ARTICLE VI

All persons being accused of a specific crime, which

---

43 Qur'an 4:58

44 Qur'an 42:38

must be supported by a court warrant, will have their constitutional rights as outlined in ARTICLE II temporarily suspended and replaced with the following rights:

Right to Presumption of Innocence

All persons accused are considered innocent until proven guilty. The burden of proof falls upon the accuser. No detainee may be held for longer than 24 hours unless a court order for further detainment is obtained based on the assessment of credible evidence related to the charges brought forth. No detainee may be subjected to physical or psychological torture, and/or humiliation, and/or forced confession, and/or any other form of physical or psychological harm or abuse. If the court finds the accused innocent of the charges put forth, then no further legal proceedings or accusations on the same case may be presented.[45]

Right to a Fair and Speedy Trial

All persons accused of a crime have the right to a fair trial that shall be free of prejudice, influence, or any external factors that may cause injustice to occur. The accused also has the right to be tried quickly without undue delay.[46]

Right to an Attorney

All persons accused of a crime shall have the right to be represented through a specialized attorney if they should so chose. If an attorney cannot be arranged or afforded by the accused, then it is the responsibility of the republic to provide an attorney with no expenses to the accused.[47]

---

45 Qur'an 10:68, 24:11, 49:12

46 Qur'an 4:58

47 Qur'an 26:12-14

Punishment does not exceed the Crime Committed

The court is responsible for ensuring that all punishments and rulings decreed by its judges are less than or equal to the nature of the crime committed. Therefore, excessive bail shall not be required, nor excessive fines imposed, nor cruel and unreasonable punishments inflicted.[48]

Right of Confrontation

Any person being accused has the right to face his/her accusers.[49]

Right to Appeal

All persons have the right to appeal a ruling that is found to be against them by requesting that a new trial be set with a different judge presiding. An appeal may only be carried out one time, unless it can be proven through credible evidence that both trials did not display fairness or a full analysis of facts, in which case the high court will preside over the matter, and their judgment supersedes all other judgments and shall be final.[50]

ARTICLE VII

Government shall be funded through the revenue generated from the legal sale of the natural public resources, as well as the revenue generated by government through services and/or taxation.

ARTICLE VIII

All branches of the government of the republic shall operate in complete transparency and openness. Records must be made public, and meetings of the national council

---

48 Qur'an 16:126

49 Qur'an 49:12

50 Qur'an 21:78-79

shall be deliberated to an open audience, and/or through a televised screening.[51]

The only exception to this transparency requirement shall be matters that are deemed threatening to the security of the republic and/or the general well-being of its citizens, and, in such cases, the records of deliberations of the kind may be concealed from the public for a maximum period of one year, to be extended only with the approval of the high court, for a maximum period not exceeding ten years.[52]

Article ix

Government officials, government employees and elected national council members, shall not hold any other position or title while serving in government or on the national council.

All government officials, government employees, and elected national council members shall be obligated to take the oath of the republic before commencing their duties:

> Oath of the republic: "I [name of person to be placed here] solemnly swear before God and before the witness of the citizens of this republic to uphold the role of [position to be placed here] to the best of my abilities to protect the integrity of the constitution and the republic. I swear to live my life according to the laws and regulations of the republic and to uphold the highest moral character. I swear to work in the best interest of the republic and to constantly strive to improve life for its citizens. I swear never to abuse my position or authority in any way, shape or form for personal gain. I swear never to carry favor to any person or group or entity beyond what is fair and just. I swear to stand for and to promote the

---

51 Qur'an 58:9-10

52 Qur'an 58:9

laws of peace and justice and equality wherever I
may be. I have placed God as a witness over this
oath of mine, may He have mercy on my soul and
guide me to always do what is right."[53]

The breaking of such oath shall be the basis for legal
proceedings and/or impeachment.

ARTICLE X
With the exception of declarations of war made by the
national council, no branch of government, or person
from within republic, may directly or indirectly finance,
sponsor, or engage in, the destabilization or undermining
of any country or nation by way of design and/or by way
of covert or otherwise armed operations.[54]

ARTICLE XI
Government shall encourage and support the pursuit
of creativity, arts, sciences, exploration, and technical
innovation within the republic.[55]

Government shall also ensure that intellectual rights be
protected from infringement and unauthorized duplication.[56]

ARTICLE XII
Amendments towards the betterment of this constitution
may be made based on a 5/6 vote of the national council and
a unanimous endorsement from the high court justices as to
the legality of the amendment in view of the existing articles
of constitution. All amendments must be listed as such and
not inserted into the original text of this constitution.[57]

In God we have placed our trust...

---

53 Qur'an 48:10

54 Qur'an 2:11-12, 2:204-205, 38:28

55 Qur'an 27:40, 34:13, 55:33

56 Qur'an 3:188

57 Qur'an 11:88

Highlights and Benefits

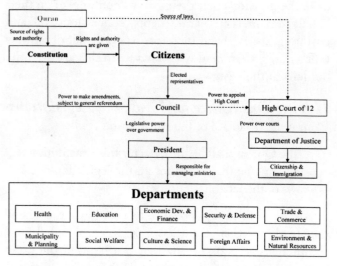

As seen in the previous chapters of this book, details have been given to the reader on the shape of the laws that would govern a republic based on the Qur'an, as well as how to deal with specific laws and everyday issues.

Below is a brief analysis of some of the points made in the constitution:

Offering a "Clean Break" from the Past
Point 1 of ARTICLE I of the constitution reads:

> "This constitution, and its subsequent laws, shall override and supersede any existing constitutions, treaties, agreements, legislations and/or laws."

This is designed to enable people/nations coming under the constitution to stand on their own two feet, free from the burdens and obligations and favors that their old regimes may have seen fit to enter into. The people of the current Islamic world have not been able for some time to participate in the shaping of their government, or in the decisions that their government makes on their behalf and in their name (debts, concessions, oil and basing rights, etc.) and therefore it is only out of fairness that a new government would have a fresh start from the burdens of the past.

Having One Source for Laws and Legislations
Point 4 of ARTICLE I of the constitution reads:

> "The Qur'an shall be the basis for this constitution and shall be the source for all the legislation and laws of the republic."

Although this may appear to be creating a 'theocracy,' the truth is that the Scripture is a detailed and comprehensive book of law that can be used the same way other nations would revert to British or International law. The benefits of using this constitution where there is a majority Muslim population, other than its just laws, is that it overcomes sectarian disputes or differing laws by the Sunnis or Shia in basing all legislation back to one single source: the Qur'an.

All Civil Freedoms Protected and Preserved
Points 1-8 of ARTICLE II of the constitution grants the following rights:

- Freedom of Speech
- Freedom of Faith
- Freedom of Movement
- Right to Privacy
- Right to Possess Wealth
- Right to Welfare
- Right against Discrimination

- Right to Seek Justice

This is where Islam has been misrepresented and misunderstood by the media and even by some of its followers. Islam both historically, and, according to the laws of the Scripture, is obligated to protect and preserve rights and freedoms of others, which includes: freedom of religion. A true Islamic republic is one in which Muslims, Christians, Jews and Atheists make up its population and are able to have equal rights and hold equal positions in private business or in government.

Government of the People

ARTICLE III of the constitution deals with the formation of an elected 'national council' which shall hold all major power for the republic and which shall be representative of all cities/towns/people irrespective of faith or ethnic background.

The idea of a national council is taken from the mode of government found in the Scripture based on consultation (known as 'shura' in Arabic) as well as the concept of representation in the Scripture for large groups of people.

Legislation Made Through Consultation

Point 1 of the powers granted to the national council in ARTICLE III reads:

> "The power to make, review, amend, and repeal laws in accordance with the principles of justice"

All legislation made by the national council will be subject to debate and discussion until a 2/3 majority (that may include people of various faiths and beliefs) are convinced that such law is in line with the principles of justice.

Tax is capped at 20 Percent

Point 7 of the powers granted in ARTICLE III of the constitution reads:

> "The power to stipulate taxation for individuals and corporations, on condition that such taxation does not exceed 20 percent."

While many of the Islamic countries today are currently in possession of vast oil wealth, there may be no need for any taxation laws (except for goods and imports) for some years or decades. However, when the government does decide to pass tax laws, there is a cap of 20 percent derived from the reference in the Scripture to all income. The word "ghana'im" as used in the Scripture refers to any revenue generated, and not only that which is gained from wars as the Sunnis claim (the Sunni belief is that tax is only 2.5 percent as derived from the Hadith books, while the Shia have correctly understood the 20 percent requirement, however, they have decided to pay it to their religious leaders rather than to their government).

The 20 percent tax limit makes a world of difference when compared to governments who tax their populations or corporations sometimes up to 50 percent.

Protecting the Value of Money

Point 9 of the powers granted in ARTICLE III of the constitution reads:

> "The power to coin money as legal tender, only if such money is coined in gold or silver or backed by gold or silver."

The world has been accustomed to using 'fiat' money for the past 3-4 decades (that is money which is not backed by anything tangible); however, the Scripture stipulates that value must be retained at all times in money by having it backed by gold and silver. This does not mean that people must once again start carrying gold or silver coins (though that is possible), but it does mean that the paper in your hand must have real value by only allowing its issuance if the gold or silver that backs it exists and can be claimed.

Although this move might appear to be economically regressing, the people who have undergone wars or political upheavals know that the value of money is illusionary when dealing with fiat money, and that the millions they once had in the banks or which they held in cash (and could buy homes or cars with) suddenly could not afford to buy them a dinner to feed their family!

Having money backed by gold and silver is ethically, politically and economically the soundest form of business and the one that protects peoples rights as well as deters from inflation (inflation being primarily caused by printing more and more fiat money).

Interest Free Society
Point 10 of the powers granted in ARTICLE III of the constitution reads:

> "The power to lend and/or borrow money, interest free, on behalf of the republic."

Interest has been completely prohibited by the Scripture as it falls into the area of 'deceit' and of robbing the people from their belongings by way of false logic and trickery. While interest may appear to make sense (you are lending out your money and deserve something in return), it is a logical fallacy since the interest being repaid does not exist to begin with and thus can never be repaid.

Wildlife Conservation

Point 12 of the powers granted in ARTICLE III of the constitution reads:

> "The power to preserve and protect wildlife and the natural ecological balance."

A tenet of the Scripture is that we work with our environment so that it will continue to support and provide for us. A nation which does not force itself to be environmentally conscious is not only harming itself, but is also harming its neighbors and the other inhabitants of the Earth who live and breath the same air and sit under the same sun and moon.

Helping Other People/Nations

Points 19, 20 and 21 of the powers granted in ARTICLE III of the constitution read:

> "The power to mediate, through peaceful means, an end to armed conflict in/or between foreign nations.
>
> The power to aid and/or assist oppressed people in foreign nations, by granting them asylum and/or negotiating on their behalf, on condition that they have requested such help.
>
> The power to provide humanitarian aid and/or assistance for crisis relief of any foreign nation and/or people in need."

The Scripture requires the republic not to be selfish and inward, but also to turn outward to end disputes, give asylum and help to the oppressed, and give aid and humanitarian services to those in need.

War Only In Self Defense

Point 22 of the powers granted in Article iii of the constitution reads:

> "The power to declare war and appropriate a war cabinet if the republic is under physical attack, and/or economic attack, and/or if its security and/or citizens are under an imminent and recognizable threat of attack."

No Islamic republic can declare war on its neighbors or any other people/nation unless it is first attacked —physically by war machines or troops, and/or economically by a blockade or undermining the economic life source(s) of the republic, or if it is clear that it will be imminently attacked. Waging war for glory or territorial expansion or simply to keep the population distracted is against the principles of justice and the laws of the Scripture.

An Independent Judicial System

Article v of the constitution reads:

> "The judicial powers of the republic shall be vested in an independent high court and its subsequent lower courts that shall judge according to the laws as placed by the national council."

The most important reason for having the three branches of government (legislative, executive, and judicial) is to create the environment for 'justice' to prevail without having to worry about the president or any other branch of government swaying the decision regarding defendants one way or the other for political or any other reasons.

Rights of Defendants Guaranteed

Points 1-6 of ARTICLE VI of the constitution grant defendants the following rights:

- Right to Presumption of Innocence
- Right to a Fair and Speedy Trial
- Right to an Attorney
- Punishment does not exceed the Crime Committed
- Right of Confrontation
- Right to Appeal

The justice system is the main pillar of an Islamic-based constitution and the right for people to seek such justice against wrongdoing is guaranteed with none being above the law.

Transparency and Openness of Government

ARTICLE VIII of the constitution reads:

> "All branches of the government of the republic shall operate in complete transparency and openness. Records must be made public, and meetings of the council shall be deliberated to an open audience, and/or through a televised screening."

The constitution demands that the government acts honestly and openly at all times with nothing to hide from its people. Open meetings, open transcripts, known objectives, clear agendas, etc. are all part of and integral to the society and republic.

No Favor beyond What Is Just

Article ix of the constitution reads:

> "Oath of the republic: 'I [name of person to be placed here] solemnly swear before God and before the witness of the citizens of this republic to uphold the role of [position to be placed here] to the best of my abilities to protect the integrity of the constitution and the republic. I swear to live my life according to the laws and regulations of the republic and to uphold the highest moral character. I swear to work in the best interest of the republic and to constantly strive to improve life for its citizens. I swear never to abuse my position or authority in any way, shape or form for personal gain. I swear never to carry favor to any person or group or entity beyond what is fair and just. I swear to stand for and to promote the laws of peace and justice and equality wherever I may be. I have placed God as a witness over this oath of mine, may He have mercy on my soul and guide me to always do what is right.'"

The oath of the republic is a requirement to be taken by each and every government employee or council member. The oath is binding by law and is designed to ensure that all those working in government maintain the utmost ethical standards and responsibility. The oath forbids favors being given to individuals, groups, or entities beyond what they rightly deserve under the law and by the constitution. This limits the ability of pressure groups and/or corporations to shape the decisions of government to their favor while undermining the true needs and rights of the individual.

Secret Services, Espionage, and Covert Operations Forbidden

ARTICLE X of the constitution reads:

> "With the exception of declarations of war made by the national council, no branch of government, or person from within republic, may directly or indirectly finance, sponsor, or engage in, the destabilization or undermining of any country or nation by way of design and/or by way of covert or otherwise armed operations."

The constitution forbids any 'intelligence' type of organization to exist that is dedicated to undermining and disrupting other people/nations in order to benefit the mother state. An Islamic republic is one that respects the right/privacy of its people as well as the right/privacy of others to govern themselves as they see fit and without becoming the 'hand of fate' that swings the balance to its favor.

Creativity and Science Encouraged

ARTICLE XI of the constitution reads:

> "Government shall encourage and support the pursuit of creativity, arts, sciences, exploration, and technical innovation within the republic."

The Scripture is a book that promotes the arts and sciences and which is always challenging mankind to explore the earth and the heavens and see the evidence of the past and to drive towards the future. As such, the constitution recognizes this call to creativity and has made it an integral part of the constitution to be promoted and protected.

Changes for the Better

ARTICLE XII of the constitution reads:

> "Amendments towards the betterment of this constitution may be made based on a 5/6 vote of the national council and a unanimous endorsement from the high court justices as to the legality of the amendment in view of the existing articles of constitution. All amendments must be listed as such and not inserted into the original text of this constitution."

Since God is the only 'absolute perfection' in our human minds, then it is only sensible to recognize that there may be shortcomings or gaps in this proposed constitution which will be filled at a later stage and time by the people who have chosen it to be their source document.

15

Spirituality in Islam— Salat

The word "Salat" and its derivatives occur in the Scripture over 70 times and is emphasized by God Almighty as a critical aspect for the spiritual development and progress of believers.

According to the Sunnis and Shia, the Salat was decreed by God to the Prophet Mohammed during the night of ascension, in which God decreed 50 Salats per day, only to be reduced to 5 Salats per day due to pleading of the Prophet.

While the average Sunni or Shia may not have any problems with the above tale, it is not only blasphemous that God would not know what to decree upon His creation, but it is also historically false as God has showed us many times that all the prophets prior to Mohammed knew Salat and carried it out along with their families and followers (see 6:162, 10:87, 11:87, 14:37, 19:31, 31:17).

What is Salat?

Not only do the Sunnis and Shia distort the truth regarding the origin of Salat, but they also confuse and confound its purpose by teaching that Salat is a "ritual prayer" decreed by God to take place at specific times during the day and that non-adherence to this prayer will result in Hell-fire.

While there is no doubt that we are commanded to 'hear and obey' any and all commands from our Lord (see 2:285), we are at the same time commanded not to uphold that which we have not verified ourselves (see 17:36).

According to the Qur'an, the correct Salat is a vehicle by which help is sought and given and by which people are assisted to avoid evil and vice:

> *"And seek help through patience and through the Salat. It is a difficult thing, but not so for the humble."*
> *(Qur'an 2:45)*

> *"Recite what is inspired to you of the Book, and hold the Salat, for the Salat prohibits evil and vice; but certainly the remembrance of God is the greatest. God knows everything you do." (Qur'an 29:45)*

Can those who carry out the 'ritual prayer' claim to have achieved such goals?

The closest match for the word "Salat" is the Arabic root word "Silla" which, in its most basic form, means: 'to link/connect/bond.' Also, unlike "prayer," which is one-way in nature, the meaning of "link/connect/bond" implies a more encompassing two-way relationship, where not only are prayers made, but also answers and guidance given.

Therefore, the word Salat, using a more accurate and correct definition based on its usage in the Qur'an, would best be termed as: *"contact prayer."*

How to carry out the Salat?

To make a proper Salat requires certain steps and preparations that God has ordained with His knowledge. In this chapter we will examine the steps and details of Salat as found in the Qur'an.

A. Timing for Salat

According to the Qur'an, there are *three* Salat times that have been prescribed:

1. Salat Al-Fajr (Dawn Salat 24:58);
2. Salat Al-Wusta (Middle Salat 2:238);
3. Salam Al-Isha (Evening Salat 24:58).

> *"O you who believe, let those who are maintained by your oaths, and those who have not yet attained puberty, request your permission regarding three times: before the dawn Salat, and when you put off your attire from the noon time, and after the evening Salat. These are three private times for you. Other than these times, it is not wrong for you or them to intermingle with one another. God thus clarifies the revelations for you. And God is Knowledgeable, Wise." (Qur'an 24:58)*

> *"Maintain the Salawaat; and the middle Salat; and*

stand for God dutifully." (Qur'an 2:238)

In addition to the revealing names of each Salat which identifies its timing, we find an abundance of detail in the Qur'an giving more information to the specific starting times in which they are to be observed:

> *"And hold the Salat at the two parts of the day, and the near part of the night. The good deeds take away the bad. This is a reminder to those who remember." (Qur'an 11:114)*

> *"Hold the Salat at the zenith of the sun, until the darkening of the night; and the Qur'an at dawn; the Qur'an at dawn is witnessed." (Qur'an17:78)*

Verse 11:114 gives us the three Salat timings as 1) the first part of the day (dawn), 2) the second part of the day[58] (noon), 3) the near part of the night (evening). Verse 17:78 further defines the timing for the Wusta/Middle Salat as beginning with noon and ending with dusk/sunset - this is why the middle Salat does not carry the name of a time period, but rather a description of its position between the other two Salat.

A few observations/notes on the three Salat times:

- Although the Sunnis make a claim that there are five Salat times (as decreed by their Hadiths), they only observe three Salat using the proper protocol of having an audible voice (17:110);

- The Shia, although claiming to adhere to five Salat like the Sunnis, only hold three Salat times each day (claiming that they are permitted to join between some of the Salat times);

---

58 The day contains a minimum of three parts/edges (see 20:130).

- The Jewish Bible, in affirming the previous knowledge people have of Salat, also affirms that such a practice was carried out three times each day (Daniel 6:10, Psalms 55:16-17).

B. Ablution/Cleansing of the Body

As a preparation for Salat, an ablution is required using water, or, if not available, clean dry soil.

> "O you who believe, if you rise to hold the Salat, then wash your faces and your hands up to the elbows, and wipe your heads and your feet to the ankles; and if you have had intercourse, then you shall bathe. And if you are ill, or traveling, or you have excreted feces, or you have had sexual contact with the women, and you cannot not find water, then you shall select from the clean soil; you shall wipe your faces and your hands with it. God does not want to place any hardship on you, but He wants to cleanse you and to complete His blessings upon you that you may be thankful." (Qur'an 5:6)

C. Be of a Clear Mind

Being of a clear mind with comprehension of what is being said/done is also a requirement of Salat.

> "O you who believe, do not approach the Salat while you are intoxicated, until you know what you are saying. Nor if you have had intercourse, unless traveling, until you bathe. And if you are ill, or traveling, or one of you has excreted feces, or you had sexual contact with the women, and could not find water, then you shall select from the clean soil; you shall wipe your faces and hands. God is Pardoning, Forgiving." (Qur'an 4:43)

D. Be in a Stationary Standing Position

The normal mode for achieving the Salat is to be in a stationary standing position. However, if there are impeding circumstances, then a person may attempt to achieve the Salat while walking or riding.

> "Maintain the Salawaat; and a balanced Salat; and stand for God dutifully. But if you are in a state of fear, then you may do so while walking or riding. If you become secure, then remember God as He has taught you what you did not know." (Qur'an 2:238-239)

E. Use a Moderate Voice, Recite the Qur'an

Using words from the Qur'an is a 'key' to helping a person achieve the state of Salat. Various phrases may be read out from the Scripture, or various verses, each depending on the need and situation of the person conducting the Salat. Some verses are in the form of a plea, while others are an invocation upon God to assist and to protect from the devil and his whispers/influence. There is no right or wrong in which verses to select. Each verse from the Qur'an has its own unique aspects and its own unique purpose.

> "Say: 'Call on God or call on the Almighty; by whichever you call on, to Him are the best names.' And do not be too loud in making your Salat, nor too quiet; but seek a path in between." (Qur'an 17:110)

> "Recite what is inspired to you of the Book, and hold the Salat, for the Salat prohibits evil and vice; but certainly the remembrance of God is the greatest. God knows everything you do." (Qur'an 29:45)

"You shall hold the Salat at the setting of the sun until the darkness of the night; and the Qur'an at dawn; the Qur'an at dawn is witnessed." (Qur'an 17:78)

F. Perform Two Prostrations

The normal length of a Salat is two prostrations (which may be shortened to one in a sate of fear). Each prostration by default involves kneeling to achieve the position of prostration.

"And if you are with them and you hold the Salat for them, then let a group from among them stand with you and let them bring their weapons; and when they have prostrated then let them be behind you; and let a group who has not yet made the contact prayer come and make the contact prayer with you, and let them be wary and let them bring their weapons with them. The rejecters hope that you would neglect your weapons and goods so they can come upon you in one blow. There is no sin upon you if you are impeded by rainfall, or if you are ill, that you place down your weapons. And be wary. God has prepared for the rejecters a humiliating retribution." (Qur'an 4:102)

G. End Salat With Specific Prayer

Salat is ended with a specific prayer to God outlining the Divinity and Oneness of the Almighty.

"And say: 'Praise to God who has not taken a son, nor does He have a partner in sovereignty, nor does He have an ally out of weakness.' And glorify Him greatly." (Qur'an 17:111)

Believers vs. Submitters

While there is no doubt that any person may attempt to perform Salat as he/she wishes, a study of the Scripture reveals that the main people who will be successful at making the Salat on a regular basis are ones who have advanced to the stage of being Mumins (believers).

> *"O you who believe, do not approach the Salat while you are intoxicated, until you know what you are saying. Nor if you have had intercourse, unless traveling, until you bathe. And if you are ill, or traveling, or one of you has excreted feces, or you had sexual contact with the women, and could not find water, then you shall select from the clean soil; you shall wipe your faces and hands. God is Pardoning, Forgiving." (Qur'an 4:43)*

> *"So, when you have done the Salat, then remember God while standing, or sitting, or on your sides. So, when you are relieved, then hold the Salat. Indeed, the Salat for the believers is a timed schedule." (Qur'an 4:103)*

While most people may not realize the difference, the Scripture has made a clear distinction between "Muslims" (those who simply have submitted to God) and "Mumins" (those who have advanced and strive with their wealth and lives in the sake of God):

> *"The Nomads said: 'We believe (Amana).' Say: "You have not believed; but you should say: 'We have submitted (Aslamna)', for belief has not yet entered into your hearts." If you obey God and His messenger, He will not put any of your works to waste. God is Forgiver, Merciful. Believers (Muminoon) are those who believe in God and His messenger, then they became without doubt, and*

THE NATURAL REPUBLIC

*they strive with their money and their lives in the cause
of God. These are the truthful ones." (Qur'an 49:14–15)*

Therefore, if you are not able to benefit from Salat,
do not despair, the benefits will come eventually when
you have calmed your mind through patience and have
nourished your soul through good works.

Other Issues

Being in Groups or Alone
Salat may be performed in groups or in an individual basis.

> *"And if you are with them and you hold the Salat for
> them, then let a group from among them stand with
> you and let them bring their weapons; and when they
> have prostrated then let them be behind you; and let a
> group who has not yet made the contact prayer come
> and make the contact prayer with you, and let them
> be wary and let them bring their weapons with them.
> The rejecters hope that you would neglect your weapons
> and goods so they can come upon you in one blow. There
> is no sin upon you if you are impeded by rainfall, or if
> you are ill, that you place down your weapons. And be
> wary. God has prepared for the rejecters a humiliating
> retribution." (Qur'an 4:102)*

> *"The angels called to him while he was standing,
> making contact (YuSali), in the temple enclosure:
> 'God gives you glad tidings of John, authenticating
> the word from God, and a master, and steadfast, and
> a prophet from the upright.'" (Qur'an 3:39)*

Friday/Jum'a Salat
One issue which arises from time to time is that of the
Jum'a (Friday) Salat. The establishment of a Salat similar

to the Jewish "Sabaath" is based on a misconception of verse 62:9 which speaks of the importance of Salat even if people are gathered together, and does not establish a 7-day week in which Friday is a special day!

> "O you who believe, when the Salat is called to on the day of assembly, you shall hasten towards the remembrance of God, and cease all selling. This is better for you, if only you knew." (Qur'an 62:9)

Beware!

The benefits from being able to commune with the One true God and receive direct feedback and/or answers to prayers cannot be emphasized enough. It is for this reason that we must all be aware that the devil and his followers have this vehicle in their sights and that severing the communion with God and rendering the act to a an empty ritual has and will continue to be a priority item (cutting us off at the source):

> *"The devil only wants to cause strife between you through intoxicants and gambling, and to repel you away from remembering God and from the Salat. Will you be deterred?" (Qur'an 5:91)*

> *"Then generations came after them who lost the Salat, and followed desires. They will find their consequences." (Qur'an 19:59)*

Now that we have found the Salat once again, will we discard our ability to commune with God and turn the Salat into mindless empty rituals as the generations before us have done?

Will we be deterred?

16

Spirituality in Islam—Fasting

As we have already shown in chapter 13, the correct Islamic calendar is a luni-solar one which has its first month beginning on the full moon that occurs on or immediately after the Winter Solstice—Ramadhan.

This makes the month of fasting occur around December of each year on the Gregorian calendar.

[Yusuf Ali Translation 2:185] Ramadhan is the (month) in which was sent down the Qur'an, as a guide to mankind, also clear (Signs) for guidance and judgment (Between right and wrong). So every one of you who is present (at his home) during that month should spend it in fasting, but if any one is ill, or on a journey, the prescribed period (Should be made up) by days later. Allah intends every facility for you; He does not want to put to difficulties. (He wants you) to complete the prescribed period, and to glorify Him in that He has guided you; and perchance ye shall be grateful.

[Yusuf Ali Translation 97:1-5] We have indeed revealed this (Message) in the Night of Power: And what will explain to thee what the night of power is? The Night of Power is better than a thousand months. Therein come down the angels and the Spirit by Allah's permission, on every errand: Peace!... This until the rise of morn!

Such an understanding fits perfectly with the information that the Qur'an was revealed on a specific night in that specific month (i.e. the special night was when the Earth stood at a specific location in relation to the sun and the moon and the universe, and such night would only be repeated when the Earth returns to exactly the *same* location—which is only possible in a Solar based system). Therefore, the problem created by Muslims today using a wildly spinning calendar is that this special night and the month it is based in are moving incoherently from summer to winter to autumn.

Who is the Audience?

The predominant view held by the Sunnis and Shia is that fasting is a requirement of every male and female Muslim from youth and until death, and that the fast is one of the pillars that make up traditional Islam and cannot be forsaken or abandoned.

> *"O you who believe, fasting has been decreed for you as it was decreed for those before you, perhaps you may be righteous. A few number of days; however, if any of you is ill or traveling, then the same number from different days; and as for those who can do so but with difficulty, they may redeem by feeding the needy. And whoever does good voluntarily, then it is better for him. And if you fast it is better for you if only you knew." (Qur'an 2:183-184)*

As pointed out with the subject of Salat, the audience for the act is not the population in general or even the Muslims/Submitters; rather, it is decreed upon the 'Mumineen/Believers' who are set upon attaining a higher reward due to their dedication to the cause of God alone.

> *"The Nomads said: 'We believe* (Amana).*' Say: "You have not believed; but you should say: 'We have submitted* (Aslamna)',*for belief has not yet entered into your hearts." If you obey God and His messenger, He will not put any of your works to waste. God is Forgiver, Merciful. Believers* (Muminoon) *are those who believe in God and His messenger, then they became without doubt, and they strive with their money and their lives in the cause of God. These are the truthful ones." (Qur'an 49:14-15)*

Why Fast?

The importance of the fast in Ramadhan can be seen in its relation to the special "Night of Decree" which occurs in that particular month and in which the month is blessed by God sending His angels and Spirit to carry out His commands.

> "We have sent it down in the Night of Decree. And do you know what is the Night of Decree? The Night of Decree is better than one thousand months. The angels and the Spirit come down in it with the permission of their Lord to carry out every matter. It is peaceful until the coming of dawn." (Qur'an 97:1-5)

> "We have sent it down in a blessed night. Surely, We were to warn. In it, is a decree for every matter of wisdom." (Qur'an 44:3-4)

It is this significant and major event that calls for a time of reflection and purification.

How Many Days is the Fast?

Islamic scholars have determined that fasting shall be for a full lunar month based on verse 2:185 (where it says, "Whoever from you is witness to that month, then let him fast in it"). However, the length of the fast has already been established in verses 2:183-184, which they conveniently overlooked:

> "O you who believe, fasting has been decreed for you as it was decreed for those before you, perhaps you may be righteous. A few number of days; however, if any of you is ill or traveling, then the same number from different days; and as for those who can do so but with difficulty, they may redeem by feeding the needy. And whoever does good voluntarily, then it is better for

him. And if you fast it is better for you if only you knew." (Qur'an 2:183-184)

Ignoring the fact that neither Jews nor Christians record a 30-day obligatory fasting period (the Jews record Yom Kippur as being the day of fasting which concludes the Ten Days of Repentance), the Scripture clarifies the period when we are to fast by the word "madoodat," which means "few." This word typically indicates a number from three to ten as the term *"madoodat"* is used for numbers, which can be simply counted by the fingers of the hand (this same word can be seen in verse 2:203 to indicate a period of three days).

The answer (which number is it from three to ten?) is derived from verse 2:185, in which God says "so that you may complete the count." The complete count for our number system is a system based on sets of 10 (see 2:196). For instance, when we reach ten, we start the count again with 11, 12, 13, etc. (this is different from an eight-based system that has been used in the past or even a seven-based system).

Therefore: Fasting = Ten days

This would be any ten days that occur within the month of Ramadhan, unless one is ill or travelling, then he/she may substitute with ten days from a different month. (2:185).

How long is the Daily Fast?
As for the daily length of the fast, it is to occur from just before dawn and lasts until night has approached:

"It has been made lawful for you during the night of fasting to approach your women sexually. They are a garment for you and you are a garment for them. God knows that you used to betray your souls so He

has accepted your repentance, and forgiven you; now you may approach them and seek what God has written for you. And you may eat and drink until the white thread is distinct from the black thread of dawn; then you shall complete the fast until night; and do not approach them while you are devoted in the temples. These are the boundaries of God, so do not transgress them. It is thus that God clarifies His revelations to the people who they may be righteous." (Qur'an 2:187)

While the Shia maintain the correct length of the daily fast (until night), the Sunnis are clear violators of this command as they encourage the breaking of the fast at sunset due to their following of a Hadith in which the prophet is supposed to have overridden the instructions of God and told his followers to "make early" the breaking of the fast!

What is to be Abstained From?

"It has been made lawful for you during the night of fasting to approach your women sexually. They are a garment for you and you are a garment for them. God knows that you used to betray your souls so He has accepted your repentance, and forgiven you; now you may approach them and seek what God has written for you. And you may eat and drink until the white thread is distinct from the black thread of dawn; then you shall complete the fast until night; and do not approach them while you are devoted in the temples. These are the boundaries of God, so do not transgress them. It is thus that God clarifies His revelations to the people who they may be righteous." (Qur'an 2:187)

During the daylight hours of the 10-day fast, believers are to abstain from the following:

- Food
- Drink
- Sexual activity

Fasting as Expiation

Other than the ten days of Ramadhan, there are different fasts mentioned in the Qur'an as expiation for certain sins.

> *"God will not hold you for your casual oaths, but He will hold you for what oaths you have made binding; its cancellation shall be the feeding of ten poor from the average of what you feed your family, or that you clothe them, or that you free a slave; whoever cannot find such shall fast for three days; this is a cancellation for making your oaths when you swear. And be careful from making oaths. It is such that God clarifies for you His revelations that you may be thankful." (Qur'an 5:89)*

> *"And complete the Pilgrimage and the visit for God. But, if you are prevented, then make what is affordable of donation, and do not shave your heads until the donation reaches its destination; but whoever of you is ill or has an affliction to his head, then he may redeem by fasting or giving a charity or a rite. But if you are able, then whoever continues the visit until the Pilgrimage, then he shall provide what is affordable of donation; but for he who cannot find anything, then he must fast for three days during the Pilgrimage and seven when he returns; this will make a complete ten; this is for*

those whose family is not present at the Restricted Temple. And be aware of God, and know that God is severe in retribution." (Qur'an 2:196)

"And it is not for a believer to kill another believer except by mistake. And whoever kills a believer by mistake, then he shall free a believing slave, and give compensation to the family; except if they remit it. If he was from a people who are enemies to you, and he was a believer, then you shall free a believing slave. And if he was from a people with whom you have a covenant, then a compensation to his family, and free a believing slave. Whoever does not find, then the fasting of two months sequentially as a repentance from God; for God is Knowledgeable, Wise." (Qur'an 4:92)

"Those among you who have estranged their women; they can never be made as their mothers, for their mothers are those who gave birth to them. Indeed, they are uttering what is strange and a falsehood. And God is Pardoner, Forgiver. Those who had estranged their women, then they retracted what they had said, they shall free a slave before they have sexual contact between them. This is to enlighten you. God is well aware of everything you do. If he cannot find any, then he shall fast two consecutive months before any sexual contact between them. If he cannot, then he shall feed sixty poor people. That is so you would believe in God and His messenger. And these are the boundaries set by God. The disbelievers have incurred a painful retribution." (Qur'an 58:2-4)

These fasts range from a three day fast to a sixty day consecutive fast depending on the sin:

- Fasting for three days for breaking an intentional oath (if he/she was not able to feed ten poor, or clothe them, or free a slave);

- Fasting for ten days for not being able to provide the animal sacrifice during the pilgrimage (to be split as three days during the pilgrimage and seven upon the return home);

- Fasting two consecutive months in the case of manslaughter (if he/she was not able to set free a believing slave or compensate the victims family);

- Fasting for two consecutive months for those who estrange their wives (if he was not able to free a slave).

17

Spirituality in Islam— Charity

Giving charity is one of the most spoken about aspects in the Qur'an as a form of purifying the 'self' from greed. This chapter will share with the reader the forms of charity available in the Qur'an as well as its intended recipients.

> *"O you who believe, spend from what We have provided for you before a Day comes when there is no trade, nor friendship, nor intercession; and the disbelievers are the wicked." (Qur'an 2:254)*

In our study of the Qur'an, we find three forms of charity that have been stipulated:

1. Al-Khums – an obligatory 20 percent tax.

2. Sadaqa – an expiation charity.

3. Zakat – an optional charity.

Al-Khums (20 percent tax)

> "And know that anything you profit, one-fifth (Al-Khums) shall go to God and the messenger, and the relatives, and the orphans, and the poor, and the wayfarer. You will do this if you believe in God and in what We revealed to Our servant on the Day of the Criterion, the day the two armies clashed; and God is capable of all things." (Qur'an 8:41)

Sunni scholars (to support their 2.5 percent tax derived from the books of Hadith) have argued that verse 8:41 is not a general tax but that it is specific to spoils of war and does not apply to all income. Shia scholars on the other hand have understood it to apply as a tax to all income (with the twist that such tax is paid to the family of the Prophet 'Ahlul-Bayt').

A review of the subject shows that the Shia understanding is the more correct one as the word 'Ghanaim' can refer to any gain, especially that the verse clarifies itself further with the phrase 'anything you profit' (ma ghanimtum min shai).

Timing of the Tax

> "And He is the One Who initiated gardens; both trellised and untrellised; and palm trees, and plants, all with different taste; and olives and pomegranates, similar and not similar. Eat from its fruit when it blossoms and give its due on the day of harvest; and do not waste. He does not like the wasteful." (Qur'an 6:141)

The Qur'an stipulates that any dues shall be paid on "the day of harvest" which would differ from person to person each depending on his/her profession. A farmer does not have just one day of harvest in a year, but he/she would have several depending on the crops and the climate. Likewise, a lawyer or office worker receives his/her harvest on a monthly basis in the form of a salary, while a laborer may receive his/her harvest weekly in the form of a wage. Therefore, the time that the tax is due is different for each person and is calculated on the net income of the person rather than the gross (keeping in-line with the word "Ghanaim" meaning "profit").

Recipients of the Tax

> *"And know that anything you profit, one-fifth* (Al-Khums) *shall go to God and the messenger, and the relatives, and the orphans, and the poor, and the wayfarer. You will do this if you believe in God and in what We revealed to Our servant on the Day of the Criterion, the day the two armies clashed; and God is capable of all things." (Qur'an 8:41)*

There are six recipients of this tax which are identified in 8:41 with the following order of succession:

1. God — all monies spent in the cause of God.

2. The messenger—with the death of the messenger this could be construed as 'the State' (i.e. 'those in authority')[59] as long as it ruled by the laws that the messenger delivered.

3. The relatives—each according to his/her own situation.

---

59 Qur'an 4:59

4. The orphans—the needy from them.

5. The poor—self explanatory.

6. The wayfarer—those suffering from set-back due to travel.

Sadaqa (expiation charity)

"And complete the Pilgrimage and the visit for God. But, if you are prevented, then make what is affordable of donation, and do not shave your heads until the donation reaches its destination; but whoever of you is ill or has an affliction to his head, then he may redeem by fasting or giving a charity (Sadaqa) *or a rite. But if you are able, then whoever continues the visit until the Pilgrimage, then he shall provide what is affordable of donation; but for he who cannot find anything, then he must fast for three days during the Pilgrimage and seven when he returns; this will make a complete ten; this is for those whose family is not present at the Restricted Temple. And be aware of God, and know that God is severe in retribution." (Qur'an 2:196)*

"O you who believe, if you wish to hold a private meeting with the messenger, you shall offer a charity (Sadaqa) *before you do so. This is better for you, and purer. If you cannot do so, then God is Forgiver, Merciful." (Qur'an 58:12)*

"Take from their money a charity (Sadaqa) *to purify them and develop them with it, and make contact with them; for your contact is a tranquility for them; and God is Hearer, Knowledgeable. Did they not know that it is God who accepts*

repentance from His servants, and He takes the charities (Sadaqaat), *and that God is the Pardoner, Merciful." (Qur'an 9:103-104)*

This charity is expiation (penance) and is available to cover a wide range of affairs, from requesting a private meeting with the messenger to being unable to shave ones hair during the pilgrimage.

Recipients of Sadaqa

"Indeed, the charities (Sadaqaat) *are for the poor, and the needy, and those who work to collect them, and those whose hearts have been united, and to free the slaves, and those in debt, and in the cause of God, and the wayfarer. A duty from God, and God is Knowledgeable, Wise." (Qur'an 9:60)*

There are eight recipients of this charity which are identified in verse 9:60 with the following order of succession:

1. The poor.
2. The needy.
3. Those who work to collect them — the charity workers.
4. Those whose hearts have been united — recent converts.
5. To free the slaves.
6. Those in debt.
7. In the cause of God.
8. The wayfarer.

Rules of Sadaqa

> *"If you openly give charities* (Sadaqaat), *then it is acceptable; but if you conceal them and give them to the poor, then that is better for you. And He cancels some of your sins; and God is Expert to all that you do." (Qur'an 2:271)*

> *"Kind words and forgiveness are far better than a charity* (Sadaqa) *that is followed by harm. God is Rich, Compassionate. O you who believe, do not nullify your charities* (Sadaqaat) *with insult and harm; like the one who spends his money in vanity to show off to the people, and he does not believe in God and the Last Day. His example is like a stone on which there is dust, then it is subjected to a heavy rain which leaves it bare. They cannot do anything with what they have earned; and God does not guide the rejecting people." (Qur'an 2:263-264)*

The Sadaqa should be given in secret if possible, and must be given with good intent and without the giver harboring any animosity towards those receiving it.

Amount of Sadaqa

> *"They ask you about intoxicants and gambling. Say: 'In them is great harm, and a benefit for the people; but their harm is greater than their benefit.' And they ask you how much they are to give, say: 'The excess.' It is thus that God clarifies for you the revelations that you may think." (Qur'an 2:219)*

The Qur'an stipulates that in the subject of giving (covering all charities), the amount should be "the excess" and that a person must not be excessive so as to cause hardship to himself/herself.

Zakat (optional charity)

"Those who spend their money in the night and in the day, secretly and openly, they will have their recompense with their Lord, there is no fear over them nor will they grieve." (Qur'an 2:274)

"O you who believe, spend from what We have provided for you before a Day comes when there is no trade, nor friendship, nor intercession; and the disbelievers are the wicked." (Qur'an 2:254)

"The example of those who spend their money in the cause of God is like a seed that sprouts forth seven pods, in each pod there is one hundred seeds; and God multiplies for whoever He chooses, and God is Encompassing, Knowledgeable." (Qur'an 2:261)

"And the example of those who spend their money seeking the grace of God, and to save their souls, is like the example of a garden that is on a high ground and is subjected to a heavy rain, and because of that it produces double its crop. And if no heavy rain comes, then a light rain is enough. And God is Seer of what you do." (Qur'an 2:265)

"You are not responsible for their guidance, but it is God who will guide whoever He wishes. And whatever you spend out of goodness is for your own souls. And anything you spend should be in seeking the face of God. And whatever you spend out of goodness will be returned to you, and you will not be wronged." (Qur'an 2:272)

"Those who spend their money in the night and in the day, secretly and openly, they will have their recompense with their Lord, there is no fear over them nor will they grieve." (Qur'an 2:274)

There is no amount of words that can describe the benefits of giving charity for the sake of God. The verses above are just a 'sample' of the words contained in the Qur'an that urge all people to invest in their eternal future.

Recipients of Zakat

"They ask you what they should spend, say: 'What you spend out of goodness should go to your family and the relatives and the orphans, and the needy, and the wayfarer. And any good you do, God is fully aware of it.'" (Qur'an 2:215)

"Piety is not to turn your faces towards the east and the west, but pious is one who believes in God and the Last Day, and the angels, and the Book, and the prophets, and who gives money out of love to the relatives, and the orphans, and the needy, and the wayfarer, and those who ask, and to free the slaves; and who upholds the contact prayer, and who contributes towards purification; and those who keep their pledges when they make a pledge, and those who are patient in the face of hardship and adversity and when in despair. These are the ones who have been truthful, and these are the righteous." (Qur'an 2:177)

There are seven recipients of this charity which are identified in verses 2:215 and 2:177 with the following order of succession:

1. Family — this covers immediate family (parents, offspring, etc.).

2. Relatives.
3. The orphans.
4. The needy.
5. The wayfarer.
6. Those who ask.
7. To free the slaves.

Amount of Zakat

"They ask you about intoxicants and gambling. Say: 'In them is great harm, and a benefit for the people; but their harm is greater than their benefit.' And they ask you how much they are to give, say: 'The excess.' It is thus that God clarifies for you the revelations that you may think." (Qur'an 2:219)

"And spend in the cause of God, but do not throw your resources to disaster. And do good, for God loves those who do good." (Qur'an 2:195)

As with Sadaqa, the amount of Zakat is left to each individual to determine what is best. It is recommended however that only the "excess" be considered and that a person does not throw himself/herself in financial hardship by giving too much charity.

Rules of Zakat

"Those who spend their money in the cause of God, then they do not follow what they have spent with either insult or harm; they will have their recompense with their Lord, there is no fear over them nor will they grieve. Kind words and forgiveness are far better than a charity that is followed by harm. God is Rich, Compassionate." (Qur'an 2:262-263)

> *"O you who believe, spend from the good things that
> you have earned, and from what We have brought
> forth from the earth. And do not select the rotten out
> of it to give, while you would not take it yourselves
> unless you closed your eyes regarding it. And know
> that God is Rich, Praiseworthy." (Qur'an 2:267)*

Again, as with Sadaqa, the giving of any charity is not
to be followed with insult or harboring any animosity
towards the recipient. In-fact, if there is any fear that the
giver would follow his/her charity with harm, then it is
better in the eyes of God to simply give kind words as
charity. Also, with charity there is the element of "quality"
that needs to be maintained (i.e. you should only give
others what you would willingly take yourself, and not
what is rotten or unacceptable).

To Give or Not to Give?

If at the end of this chapter you are still in doubt as to the
benefits of giving charity or helping those less fortunate,
then perhaps a look into the future and reading the case of
those who did give and their subsequent reward by their
Lord will change your mind:

> *"As for the pious, they will drink from a cup which has
> the scent of musk. A spring from which the servants
> of God drink, it gushes forth abundantly. They fulfill
> their vows, and they fear a Day whose consequences
> are wide-spread. And they give food out of love to the
> poor and the orphan and the captive. 'We only feed
> you seeking the face of God; we do not desire from you
> any reward or thanks. We fear from our Lord a Day,
> which will be horrible and difficult.' So God shielded
> them from the evil of that Day, and He cast towards
> them a look and a smile. And He rewarded them
> for their patience with paradise and silk. They are*

reclining in it on raised couches, they do not have in it excessive sun nor bitter cold. And the shade is close upon them, and the fruit is hanging low within reach. And they are served upon with bowls of silver and glasses of crystal. Crystal laced with silver, measured accordingly. And they are given to drink in it from a cup which has the scent of ginger. A spring therein which is called 'Salsabeel'. And they are encircled with eternal children. If you see them you will think they are pearls which have been scattered about. And if you look, then you will see a blessing and a great dominion. They will have garments of fine green silk, and necklaces and bracelets from silver, and their Lord will give them a cleansing drink. 'This is the reward for you, and your struggle is appreciated.'"
(Qur'an 76:5-22)

May we all be amongst the dwellers of Paradise!

18

Pilgrimage: The Lost Legacy of Abraham

This chapter will deal with the final and most important feature of unity in the Islamic republic, and that is its ability to interact with other people and nations in order to share with them the knowledge and merits of a system that has been designed by the One in the Heavens for all His creation to live and prosper in peace and happiness.

"The first Sanctuary established for the people is the one in Bakk'a, blessed, and a guidance for the worlds. In it are clear signs: the station of Abraham. And whoever enters it will be secure. And God is owed from the people to make Pilgrimage to the Sanctuary, whoever can make a path to it. And whoever rejects, then God has no need of the worlds."
(Qur'an 3:96-97)

Every year, we see millions of Pilgrims heading towards Mecca for the annual Pilgrimage/Hajj. The Pilgrimage takes place in the Arabic month of Zul Hujja and lasts for a period of three days in which the Pilgrims perform a number of rites, one of which is being dressed in a white cloth called Ihraam while circling the Kaaba several times, running between the two stones of the Safa and Marwa and throwing pebbles at the devil.

Who is the Audience?

"And call out to the people with the Pilgrimage, they will come to you walking and on every trans-port, they will come from every deep enclosure."
(Qur'an 22:27)

The single most overlooked clue regarding Pilgrimage is the audience. Abraham was calling out to humankind and not to the believers or Muslims. This information poses a serious problem to the belief that Pilgrimage is a set of systematic rituals, as non-believers would not be able to identify with any of these rituals and would thus not carry them out.

Why Would People Gather?

> "The first Sanctuary established for the people is
> the one in Bakk'a, blessed, and a guidance for the
> worlds. In it are clear signs: the station of Abraham.
> And whoever enters it will be secure. And God is
> owed from the people to make Pilgrimage to the
> Sanctuary, whoever can make a path to it. And
> whoever rejects, then God has no need of the worlds."
> (Qur'an 3:96–97)

> "So that they may witness benefits for themselves,
> and mention the name of God in the appointed days
> over what He has provided for them of the animal
> livestock. So eat from it and feed the needy and the
> poor. Then let them complete their duties and fulfill
> their vows, and let them traverse at the ancient
> Sanctuary." (Qur'an 22:28–29)

Here are the two main reasons people would gather:

1. To witness benefits for themselves.
2. To be made aware of the system established by
   God for the people.

The first objective of Pilgrimage comes naturally from
such a large gathering of different people at an appointed
time(s) and place. This opens the door to opportunities
of trade, information exchange, cultural exchange,
networking, etc. This idea of the meeting and mixing of
people/races can be clearly seen in verse 49:13 below as
part of the decree of God for humanity:

> "O mankind, We created you from a male and female,
> and We made you into nations and tribes, that you

may know one another. Surely, the most honorable among you in the sight of God is the most righteous. God is Knowledgeable, Expert." (Qur'an 49:13)

The second objective of making Pilgrimage is to share with all humankind the system of laws, government, and teachings that God has decreed to us through the prophets (both physical and spiritual). This teaching is achieved during a period of a few days when the Pilgrims are invited to feast on the meats prepared specially for the event while the system of God Alone is openly discussed and shared with the visitors. Hence, the term "mention the name of God" is to remind those present (believers and non-believers) of our allegiances to God because of what He has made available for us on this Earth and everything else He has blessed us with.

Location of Pilgrimage

"The first Sanctuary established for the people is the one in Bakk'a, blessed, and a guidance for the worlds. In it are clear signs: the station of Abraham. And whoever enters it will be secure. And God is owed from the people to make Pilgrimage to the Sanctuary, whoever can make a path to it. And whoever rejects, then God has no need of the worlds." (Qur'an 3:96-97)

Unfortunately, many people have taken for granted what the Scripture actually says on this and many other subjects and hence they end up following the teachings of the sects when it comes to the system of God.

The Scripture gives the clear name Bakk'a (not Mecca) as being the location for the Pilgrimage.

Where is Bakk'a?

> [Psalm 84:4-8] Blessed are they that dwell in
> thy house: they will be still praising thee. Selah.
> Blessed is the man whose strength is in thee; in
> whose heart are the ways of them. Who passing
> through the valley of Baca make it a well; the
> rain also fills the pools. They go from strength to
> strength, every one of them in Zion appears before
> God. O Lord God of hosts, hear my prayer: give
> ear, O God of Jacob. Selah.

The name Bakk'a has been retained in ancient
scriptures and is the given as the name of the area which
is reached as pilgrims exited the valley of Rephaim from
the southwest that led to mount Zion in the heart of
Jerusalem (Samuel 5:22-23).

In-fact, the name Bakk'a is still retained for that very
same area that approaches the heart of Jerusalem from the
south west.

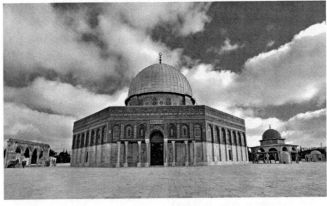

Photograph of Jerusalem (Dome of the Rock)—The first Sanctuary

This evidence of Bakk'a being Jerusalem is bizarrely
supported by Islamic history itself, which records that the

Prophet, while in Medina, used to perform the communion (Salat) towards Jerusalem for a number of years, but then the focal point (Qibla) was changed away from Jerusalem (until today, the Muslims refer to Jerusalem as the *first* of the two Qiblas —Uwla Al Qiblatain).

The Change in Focal Point (Qibla)

The source of all the confusion that has occurred seems to have been caused by the change in the Qibla (focal point) during the time of the Prophet:

> *"The foolish from among the people will say: 'What has turned them away from the focal point that they were on?' Say: 'To God are the east and the west, He guides whomsoever He wishes to a straight path.' And as such, We have made you a balanced nation so that you may be witness over the people, and that the messenger may be witness over you. And We did not make the focal point that you became on except to distinguish who follows the messenger from those who will turn on their heels. It was a great thing indeed except for those whom God had guided; God was not to waste your belief. God is Merciful and Compassionate over the people." (Qur'an 2:142-143)*

According to traditional history, the Muslims were focused on the original Qibla of Jerusalem. Then, after some time, God suddenly gave a new decree that told them to face "away" from that Qibla. This change in Qibla is supported with the verses of the Scripture in 2:142 and 2:143, and is further supported by archeological evidence that existed in the city of Medina of a mosque (masjid) with two Qibla directions (one towards Jerusalem and one opposite to Jerusalem—assumed to be towards Mecca).

The Sunnis and Shia claim that the command was for the Prophet to now face Mecca—Arabia as the permanent Qibla. However, what the sects fail to explain is why the Prophet was facing Jerusalem to begin with, especially if the Temple was located in Mecca—Arabia all along as per their claims?

Digging deeper into this issue, we find that the sectarian argument that Mecca—Arabia was being faced in this change of Qibla holds no water as turning away from Jerusalem would not put the Muslims on a path with such a supposed location:

By drawing an imaginary line from Medina to Jerusalem, we find that Mecca Arabia is off by a large distance—thus refuting the argument that Mecca was the intended focus point of the new Qibla.

What further raises suspicion that the Qibla was simply shifted 'away' from Jerusalem and not towards any city in particular (especially not Mecca—Arabia) is that the original mosque with two Qiblas has been demolished by the Saudi government and a new one built with a possible realignment done towards Mecca—Arabia.

The Final Qibla

While the initial change in Qibla may have caused the confusion for people to lean towards the location of Mecca—Arabia, it seems that most commentators have missed the verses which speak of reverting of the Qibla back to the Restricted Temple (Jerusalem).

> *"We see the shifting of your face towards the heaven; We will thus set for you a focal point that will be pleasing to you: 'You shall set yourself towards the Restricted Temple; and wherever you may be, you shall all set yourselves towards it.' Those who have been given the Book know it is the truth from their Lord. And God is not unaware of what you do."*
> (Qur'an 2:144)

The sectarian commentators of the Scripture tried to promote the idea that the change that God speaks about in verse 2:144 was the original one from Jerusalem to the Restricted Temple (which they make to be Mecca —Arabia). The problem with this argument is that it ignores the fact that in verse 2:142 God announces that a change has already taken place and that the foolish amongst the people will comment saying: "What made them change from their Qibla?" (i.e. there was a Qibla-1 which is the original, and a Qibla-2 which has sparked the questions).

Then in replying to the people in verse 2:143, the answer of God is given for the reason for the change by saying "it was a test to distinguish the true followers of the Prophet."

Finally, after this sequence, we are told that the Prophet has been directed in verse 2:144 to make the Restricted Temple his permanent Qibla (which cannot be Mecca –Arabia because there has already been one change of Qibla away from Jerusalem and towards the opposite location).

237

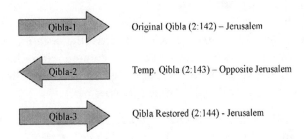

Qibla-1   Original Qibla (2:142) – Jerusalem

Qibla-2   Temp. Qibla (2:143) – Opposite Jerusalem

Qibla-3   Qibla Restored (2:144) - Jerusalem

The only way to explain the current state of Islam (giving priority to Mecca—Arabia) is that the change back to Jerusalem did not take place until very near the end of the mission of the Prophet and that he died shortly afterwards whereby the Muslims fragmented and entered into several civil wars, as per the Islamic history books. The victors from these conflicts managed to maintain the power base in Arabia and declared that the temple located in what later became known as 'Mecca Arabia' was the place where the Sanctuary established by Abraham is found and is the location of the Pilgrimage.

This would also explain why there is some archaeological confusion in why the construction of some early mosques had the facing of the Qibla to be far to the north of Mecca, while even some of the early Muslims such as Abdul-Malik Bin Marwan believed that Jerusalem was the true Qibla and center for Pilgrimage and proceeded to expand the building of the Dome of the Rock by 691AD into the architectural masterpiece that it is today.

Mecca in the Qur'an

More importantly, with regards to Mecca, we find that the Qur'an does indeed refer to a city/town by such name and that such was an obstacle for Pilgrims who were trying to make their way to the Restricted Temple in Bakk'a!

"And He is the One who withheld their hands against you, and your hands against them in the interior of Mecca, after He had made you victorious over them. God is Seer of what you do. They are the ones who rejected and barred you from the Restricted Temple, and barred your donations from reaching their destination. And there had been believing men and believing women whom you did not know, and you may have hurt them, and on whose account you would have incurred a sin unknowingly. God will admit into His mercy whoever He wills. Had they become separated, We would then have punished those from them who rejected with a painful retribution." (Qur'an 48:24-25)

This is a far cry from the claims that Mecca itself was the name of the city where the Temple is located, or that Mecca was simply another name for Bakk'a.

The Kaaba

[Pickthall Translation 5:97] Allah hath appointed the Kaba, the Sacred House, a standard for mankind, and the Sacred Month and the offerings and the garlands. That is so that ye may know that Allah knoweth whatsoever is in the heavens and whatsoever is in the Earth, and that Allah is Knower of all things.

Continuing with the sectarian history, we find that the holiest site in Mecca is the 'Kaaba' which is considered the Sanctuary of God and is the focal point for the over 1 billion Muslims worldwide. We are told that the word 'Kaaba' means a 'cube shape' and that the site in Mecca has been constructed in accordance with this design requirement.

A photo of the Sanctuary in Mecca (the Kaaba)

However, the meaning of 'cube' associated with this word is not completely accurate as the word 'Kaab/Kaaba' is associated in Arabic with any feature that is protruding, such as the bones to the side of the ankles as can be seen below:

"O you who believe, if you rise to hold the contact prayer, then wash your faces and your hands up to the elbows, and wipe your heads and your feet to the ankles (Kaabain)*; and if you have had intercourse, then you shall bathe. And if you are ill, or traveling, or you have excreted feces, or you have had sexual contact with the women, and you cannot not find water, then you shall select from the clean soil; you shall wipe your faces and your hands with it. God does not want to place any hardship on you, but He wants to cleanse you and to complete His blessings upon you that you may be thankful." (Qur'an 5:6)*

Thus, any construct, regardless of its shape can be called a 'Kaaba' as long as it stands out from the plain.

In-fact, we find that in the history of pagan Arabia, each town had its own 'Kaaba' which was a centerpiece for worship and a place for the many idols that were served alongside the One true God.

With regards to the temple area of Jerusalem, we have a 'Kaaba' in the form of the building located on the Temple Mount 'Dome of the Rock' which has been the foundation building for worship in the area for many centuries and is even considered to be the spot from which the Prophet made his journey to heaven (see 17:1).

Photograph of Jerusalem (Dome of the Rock)

The Situation of Abraham (Maqam Ibrahim)

Another feature which is noted with regards to the location of the Temple in Bakk'a is the "Maqam Ibrahim" (Station/Situation of Abraham) which we are told is to be found at the site of the Temple:

> "The first Sanctuary established for the people is the one in Bakk'a, blessed, and a guidance for the worlds. In it are clear signs: the station of Abraham. And whoever enters it will be secure. And God is owed from the people to make Pilgrimage to the Sanctuary, whoever can make a path to it. And whoever rejects, then God has no need of the worlds." (Qur'an 3:96-97)

Here we can note an apparent discrepancy for the site of Mecca where the alleged "Maqam Ibrahim" has been placed outside the alleged sanctuary/temple while it is supposed to be inside.

It seems that some early Muslims were aware of this glaring discrepancy, and as such, a solution was invented that pilgrims were to 'imagine' that the Maqam/Hijr is located inside the temple domain and thus during the Hajj the area of the Maqam/Hijr is to be walked 'around' and not 'through' just as if they are circling a continuous physical part of the temple.

With regards to explaining why the Maqam is located in the wrong place to begin with, the Muslim scholars have opted for a crude explanation whereby they claim that the Kaaba walls were destroyed by flash floods during the life of the Prophet, but that he could not muster enough money together to rebuild the Kaaba to its original size, so he opted for a smaller Kaaba leaving the Maqam outside the sanctuary!

To locate the true Maqam and its relation to the Pilgrimage, we need to explore the word as it occurs in the Scripture. The word "Maqam" occurs in the following verses: 2:125, 3:97, 5:107, 10:71, 14:14, 17:79, 19:73, 25:66, 25:76, 26:58, 27:39, 33:13, 37:164, 44:26, 44:51, 55:46, 79:40. The meanings ascribed to this word as per its usage are: "Position, status, station, situation, place."

Looking at the stories of Abraham in the Scripture and trying to find the one that is nearest in subject to the Pilgrimage rites, we come across the famous story when Abraham has a dream in which he is sacrificing his son. God in His mercy intervenes and ransoms the son of Abraham with an animal sacrifice.

> *"And when he grew enough to work with him, he said: 'My son, I am seeing in a dream that I am*

sacrificing you. What do you think?' He said: 'O my father, do what you are commanded to do. You will find me, God willing, patient.' So when they both had surrendered, and he put his forehead down. And We called him: 'O Abraham, you have carried out the vision.' It was such that We rewarded the righteous. Surely, this was an exacting test. And We ransomed him with a great animal sacrifice. And We kept his history for those who came later."
(Qur'an 37:102-108)

This episode recorded in the Scripture describes the trial/situation of Abraham with his son. Thus, for all purposes, the place where this event took place may be described as Maqam Ibrahim.

Looking back at the Temple area of Jerusalem, we find a stone outcropping underneath the Dome of the Rock where it is claimed that Abraham was about to sacrifice his son in fulfillment of 37:102-108.

Photo of the Rock within the Dome (Jerusalem)

It is also found that there are channels carved into the rock which are designed to siphon liquid to a chamber below, thus making the Maqam an ideal location for the animal sacrifice which is amongst the rites of the Pilgrimage.

Arafat—Mountain or Elevated Place?

On the subject of Arafat, we are told that this is the name of one of the mountains near Mecca —Arabia, and it is said that the Pilgrims must journey to that location as decreed in verse 2:198 and then return back to Mecca again.

> *[Pickthall Translation 2:198] "It is no sin for you that ye seek the bounty of your Lord (by trading). But, when ye press on in the multitude from 'Arafat, remember Allah by the sacred monument. Remember Him as He hath guided you, although before ye were of those astray."*

Naming a mountain Arafat and then claiming it is the one referred to in the Scripture is no great feat. However, as is becoming typical of the mistakes the Sunni and Shia scholars are making with their location for places, it is more important to ask the question: Why would people invited for Pilgrimage who are not necessarily believers perform rituals and come and go to a mountain a few kilometers away?

The obvious answer is that they would not!

The word "Arafat" in Arabic simply means "high/elevated place" (that is why the scholars have chosen a small mountain to be given this name). And, if we follow the notion that the place of Pilgrimage is the Temple Mount area, then the verse becomes crystal clear as the Temple Mount is an elevated area and hence the pilgrims who gather at the Sanctuary are by default standing at "Arafaat—the high place."

Photograph of Temple Mount in Jerusalem showing it as situated on an "elevated platform"

Safa and Marwah

> *"Indeed, the Safa and the Marwah are among the symbols of God. So whoever makes Pilgrimage to the Sanctuary, or is merely passing through, commits no error should he traverse them. And whoever donates for goodness, then God is Thankful, Knowledgeable."*
> *(Qur'an 2:158)*

The Safa and Marwah in Mecca–Arabia are two small hills/mounds between which we are told Hajar (the slave wife of Abraham) was running, searching for water after Abraham had abandoned her and her infant with no food or water. Then, while she was at the seventh run, Ismail miraculously struck his foot at the ground and a spring of water "Zamzam" burst forth!

However, the entire story of 'Abraham marrying his slave girl Hajar and then leaving her in the wilderness with Ismail based on the wishes of his wife Sarah' not only has

245

no basis whatsoever in the Book of God, but also conflicts greatly with the character of a Prophet who is devoted to God and who would never be pressured by any human into abandoning or harming another person(s). As far as we can ascertain, Abraham was married to one woman, the same woman who gave him Ismail and then, many years later, Isaac. We can also ascertain that Abraham lived near the area of the Temple (Jerusalem) and therefore would not have traveled hundreds of kilometers to carry out such an extreme act never mentioned in the Scripture of God.

With regards to the Temple area of Jerusalem, if we are looking for two protruding points, then they are easily located. The Temple area has two stone outcroppings/foundations; the first being the stone upon which lies the 'Dome of the Rock' (hence the name), while the other is a stone upon which a smaller structure has been built known as the 'Dome of the Tablets'. Thus, these two features, both of which have been preserved on the Temple Mount site, can be claimed to be the 'Safa' and 'Marwa' (the stone and the rock outcropping) that God has mentioned as being physical elements as part of the site of Pilgrimage and are amongst the symbols of God.

Summary—Highlighting Jerusalem as Bakk'a:

- Islamic history records Jerusalem as being the first focal point, or Qibla, before Mecca.

- The recipients of the Torah and Injeel (Jews and Nazarenes) acknowledge the significance of Jerusalem but deny any knowledge of Mecca.

- The name "Bakk'a" is found in the Jewish bible (see Psalms 84) as people are on their way to Jerusalem for Pilgrimage (to stand before God at Mt. Zion).

- A town by the name of 'Mecca' is mentioned

in the Qur'an as being an obstacle in the way of pilgrims to reach the Restricted Temple in Bakk'a (see Qur'an 48:24).

- Controversy and doubt over Mecca being the original site of pilgrimage has existed since the early days of Islam whereby the Kaaba in Mecca was catapulted and destroyed by an Islamic army in the days of Abdul Malik Bin Marwan while the Temple in Jerusalem was honored and upgraded.

- Physical evidence exists showing mosques built after the death of the prophet with their Qiblas (orientation) towards Jerusalem and not Mecca (see work by Cook and Crone).

- The name "Bakk'a" is still found in city maps of Jerusalem as the name of a valley located less than five miles from the Temple Mount to the southwest.

- The name "Jerusalem" (city of peace) fits the prayer of Abraham for Bakk'a to be a city of peace. (see Qur'an 2:126)

- The Scripture speaks of olives growing in the vicinity of this town where the Prophet is situated (see Qur'an 95:1-3). Olives are natural to the area of the Mediterranean (near which Jerusalem is situated) but not Arabia.

- The Qur'an tells us that the 'Maqam Ibrahim' (situation/station of Abraham) is located within the Temple at Bakk'a (see Qur'an 3:97). In Jerusalem we have the rock (upon which the dome is built) associated with the test of Abraham whereby he nearly sacrificed his son. In Mecca we have what appears to be footprints enclosed by a brass container!

- The rock over which the Dome of the Rock is situated seems designed for animals to be slaughtered on it (as evidenced by a hole in the rock which is thought to drain blood sacrifices down to a hollow cavern below). If so, then this would match perfectly the rite of Pilgrimage and the slaughter of livestock for feasting and giving to the poor/needy.

- The Kaaba is situated on an elevated area, which matches the description given in the Scripture of the Pilgrims coming to it from low/deep enclosures (see Qur'an 22:27).

- The prophecy of the Temple being re-entered (see Qur'an 17:7) when the second rise of Israel occurs can only be applicable if the Temple is under Israeli control (i.e. Jerusalem and not Mecca).

Timing of Pilgrimage

The pilgrimage is held during the three months that follow Ramadhan in the calendar year. (see chapter 13 for calendar details) and each Pilgrimage would begin with the sighting of the crescent of the moon and last until the next crescent appears (people may shorten to two days or extended beyond the sighting of the second crescent if needed).

> *"They ask you regarding the crescent moons, say: 'They are a timing mechanism for the people and the Pilgrimage.' And piety is not that you would enter a home from its back, but piety is whoever is righteous and comes to the homes from their main doors. And be aware of God that you may succeed." (Qur'an 2:189)*

"And remember God during a few number of days. Whoever hurries to two days, there is no sin upon him; and whoever delays, there is no sin upon him if he is being righteous. And be aware of God, and know that it is to Him that you will be gathered." (Qur'an 2:203)

"And complete the Pilgrimage and the visit for God. But, if you are prevented, then make what is affordable of donation, and do not shave your heads until the donation reaches its destination; but whoever of you is ill or has an affliction to his head, then he may redeem by fasting or giving a charity or a rite. But if you are able, then whoever continues the visit until the Pilgrimage, then he shall provide what is affordable of donation; but for he who cannot find anything, then he must fast for three days during the Pilgrimage and seven when he returns; this will make a complete ten; this is for those whose family is not present at the Restricted Temple. And be aware of God, and know that God is severe in retribution." (Qur'an 2:196)

Rules of Pilgrimage

Since this call is to all humankind to gather and benefit in one location, certain rules of conduct have been spelled out that must be observed by all who have agreed to attend:

"And complete the Pilgrimage and the visit for God. But, if you are prevented, then make what is affordable of donation, and do not shave your heads until the donation reaches its destination; but whoever of you is ill or has an affliction to his head, then he may redeem by fasting or giving a charity or a rite. But if you are able, then whoever continues the visit until the Pilgrimage, then he shall provide

what is affordable of donation; but for he who cannot find anything, then he must fast for three days during the Pilgrimage and seven when he returns; this will make a complete ten; this is for those whose family is not present at the Restricted Temple. And be aware of God, and know that God is severe in retribution." (Qur'an 2:196)

"The Pilgrimage months are made known. So whoever decides to perform the Pilgrimage therein, then there shall be no sexual approach, nor wickedness, nor baseless argument in the Pilgrimage. And any good that you do, God is aware of it; and bring provisions for yourselves, though the best provision is righteousness; and be aware of Me O people of understanding." (Qur'an 2:197)

"There is no sin upon you to seek goodness from your Lord. So when you disperse from the elevated place, then remember God at the symbol which is restricted, and remember Him as He has guided you; for you were straying before that." (Qur'an 2:198)

"Then you shall disperse from where the people dispersed, and seek the forgiveness of God; God is surely Forgiving, Merciful." (Qur'an 2:199)

"When you have completed your rites, then remember God as you remember your fathers or even greater. From among the people is he who says: 'Our Lord, give us from this world!' But in the Hereafter he has no part. And some of them say: 'Our Lord, give us good in this world, and good in the Hereafter, and spare us from the retribution of the Fire.' These will

have a benefit for what they have earned; and God is swift in reckoning." (Qur'an 2:200-202)

"And remember God during a few number of days. Whoever hurries to two days, there is no sin upon him; and whoever delays, there is no sin upon him if he is being righteous. And be aware of God, and know that it is to Him that you will be gathered." (Qur'an 2:203)

"And the plump livestock, We have made them for you to be among the symbols of God; you will have benefit in them. So mention the name of God upon them in succession; then, once their sides have become still, you may eat from them and feed with them the poor and the needy. It was thus that We have made them in service to you, that you may be thankful." (Qur'an 22:36)

"Neither their meat nor their blood reaches God, but what reaches Him is the righteousness from you. It was thus that He made them in service to you, so that you may glorify God for what He has guided you to, and give news to the good doers." (Qur'an 22:37)

It is thus that people would gather, be shown the ways of God, be shown the system of God, and be shown the methods of spirituality (communion) that they may pass what they have learned to others.

Other Issues

Mecca and Petra

With regards to Mecca—Arabia, during the course of this research, we are unable to find any ancient map or reference to a city in the Arabian Desert that went by the name of "Mecca" or was recorded as being on any major trading route.

However, when taking into account that the Qur'an does refer to such a town as an enemy encampment which was a deterrent to people and donations trying to make their way to the Restricted Temple located at Bakk'a (48:24-25), and that such a town has its roots in the Arabic language being the language of the Qur'an, then, in all probability, that would make the real town of Mecca mentioned in the Qur'an to be one and the same the town of Petra as the city was on a nearly direct path for any pilgrims making their way from Medina in the south to Jerusalem in the north.

It is worth noting that Petra was the center for the Nabatean people who are the originators of the Arabic language (the language used by the Qur'an) and that they had principal deities such as Laat and Uzza which are also recorded in the Qur'an:

> *"Have you considered Allaat and Al-`Uzzah? And Manaat, the third one? Do you have the males, while He has the females? What a strange distribution! These are but names that you made up, you and your forefathers. God never authorized such. They only follow conjecture, and personal desire, while the guidance has come to them from their Lord."* (Qur'an 53:19-23)

Why Did the Prophet Immigrate to Medina?

The Prophet may have been originally from either Jerusalem (Bakk'a) or Petra (Mecca) and he most likely migrated from one or both of these towns as he faced persecution for spreading the message of God Alone. It would therefore have made sense for him to emigrate south towards the town of Yathrib (Medina) as he is moving away from the jurisdiction of the Roman Empire at the time.

The relocation at Medina seems to have provided a safe-haven for the mission of the Prophet until he was ready to reclaim the Temple which was now located to his north.

What Proof is There of Previous Pilgrimages to the Temple Mount?

As Abraham has called to the Pilgrimage over 3,000 years ago, it would be logical to assume that there would be remnants/traces of previous structures or buildings on the area of the Temple Mount.

Other than the stone, which protrudes from the Temple Mount and upon which the Dome of the Rock is built, we have a historical reference that a structure did exist more than once on this same site and that the Temple was reconstructed and then was expanded by Herod in 19-20 BC. The Romans destroyed this new structure in 70 A.D. during the "War of the Jews." The archaeological proof for these claims is found in infrared images taken of the Dome of the Rock by Tuvia Sagiv (taken from paper entitled "Penetrating Insights into the Temple Mount") revealing an older pentagonal foundation beneath the current Dome of the Rock, which indicates that this site has had a function even before the Dome was built.

What about the People of the Scripture Following Different Focal Points?

> "And if you come to those who have been given the Book with every sign they will not follow your focal point, nor will you follow their focal point, nor will some of them even follow each others focal point. And if you were to follow their desires after the knowledge that has come to you, then you would be one of the wicked." (Qur'an 2:145)

Historical evidence found in the Old Testament suggests that both the Jews and Christians/Nazarenes are aware of the importance of Jerusalem:

> [Daniel 6:10] Now when Daniel knew that the writing was signed, he went into his house; and his windows being open in his chamber toward Jerusalem, he kneeled upon his knees three times a day, and prayed, and gave thanks before his God, as he did aforetime.

Archaeological evidence also confirms that synagogues from the period before and after the revelation of the Scripture were roughly oriented to face Jerusalem. (Avi-Yonah, M., Synagogue Architecture. In *Encyclopedia Judaica*, vol. 15, New York: Macmillan, 1971).

However, looking at our decreed focal-point from verse 2:144 being the "Restricted Temple" (also known as the Temple Mount, on which the Dome of the Rock is located), and not the greater area of Jerusalem or Jerusalem itself, we find that neither Jews nor Christians accept this as their orientation.

In fact, the Jews are "forbidden" from that area by their Rabbis, while the Christians seek the mount of olives nearby as their rallying point where they believe Jesus last prayed.

Clearly, as verse 2:145 suggests, there is no consensus between the Qibla of the Scripture and the Qiblas followed by the Jews and Christians/Nazarenes.

Summary of Pilgrimage

- Pilgrimage is a call to all humankind (to learn about the system of God Alone, to witness benefits for themselves, to feast);

- The location of the original Pilgrimage was at Bakk'a (Jerusalem), centering near the Temple Mount (the area on which the Dome of the

Rock is constructed);

- The timing of the Pilgrimage is during the days between the crescent moons, for a total of three Pilgrimages per year;

- During Pilgrimage, the highest moral decency shall be upheld (no improper conduct, no vileness, no baseless arguing);

- A period of feasting and feeding the poor shall follow the end of the Pilgrimage.

The time has come for Muslims to realign themselves with the Scripture of God and to call for the establishment of Jerusalem as an international city/sanctuary where all people can gather in peace and harmony for the great Pilgrimage of sharing and learning.

Perhaps the legacy of Abraham, which lives on in the Scripture, will one day be established once again.

19

The Future Starts With You

It has been our duty to warn all those to whom this message reaches of a great injustice we have all committed in the eyes of God; that is, setting up partners to our Lord God without knowing we have done so.

The enemy of humankind has said:

> *"He [Satan] said: 'For that which You have caused me to be misled, I will stalk for them on Your straight*

> *path. Then I will come to them from between their*
> *hands, and from behind them, and from their right,*
> *and from their left; and You will find most of them*
> *unthankful.'" (Qur'an 7:16-17)*

The Devil has made a solemn pledge before our Lord that he will make most of us unappreciative of God and that he will entice most of us to set up partners with our Lord, and he has been successful...

Satan has managed from the very beginning to entice our fore-parents (Adam and Eve) and have them evicted from the Garden. He managed to subdue the people of Noah, Saleh, Hud, Abraham, Moses, and Jesus making them reject God as their only Lord and Master.

And what about us, the Muslims?

Were we able to escape from the clutches of Satan?

Or, have we fallen without knowing?

> *"Say: 'Shall we inform you of the greatest losers?*
> *Those whose efforts in the worldly life were*
> *wasted while they thought they were doing good!'"*
> *(Qur'an 18:103-104)*

It is destined that many people who have set up partners with God Almighty are *not aware* of what they have done:

> *"And the Day We gather them all, then We say to the*
> *polytheists: 'Where are your partners whom you used*
> *to claim?' Then, their only excuse was to say: 'By God,*
> *our Lord, we were not polytheists!' See how they lied to*
> *themselves; and that which they invented abandoned*
> *them." (Qur'an 6:22-24)*

They will swear by God Almighty that they were not idol worshippers!

Are we all ready now to also swear?

Are we right?

The Book of God (The Scripture) is the light and guidance that we, as Muslims, must all cling to for salvation in this life and the Hereafter…

What does God Almighty have to say about His Book?

> "'Shall I seek other than God as a judge when He has sent down to you the Book fully detailed?' Those to whom We have given the Book know it is sent down from your Lord with the truth; so do not be of those who have doubt." (Qur'an 6:114)

And He said also:

> "And the word of your Lord has been completed with the truth and justice; there is no changing His words. He is the Hearer, the Knower." (Qur'an 6:115)

And again:

> "Say: 'If the sea were an inkwell for the words of my Lord, then the sea would run out before the words of my Lord run out;' even if We were to bring another like it as an extension." (Qur'an 18:109)

The Scripture is complete, detailed, has nothing left out, and does not run out of words!

Some of us may have now understood the trick that has been played on the Muslim masses by Satan and his counterparts… We *do not* need other sources such as Hadith, Sunnah, Traditions, Ulema, Imams, and/or Madhabs to complete the system of God and/or His Book. God does not accept that partners be associated with Him and that His words not be heeded.

> "These are the revelations of God, We recite them to you with the truth. So, in which narrative after God and His revelations do they believe? Woe to every sinful fabricator. He hears the revelations of God being recited to him, then he persists arrogantly, as

if he never heard them. Give him news of a painful retribution." (Qur'an 45:6–8)

Do not be arrogant when hearing the words of the Lord and do not insist on your own way after the guidance has been shown to you... It is the Devil who wishes that you deny the words of God and follow him and his allies... For such is the trap:

"And who is more wicked than he who was reminded of the revelations of his Lord but he turned away from them, and he forgot what his hands had done. We have made veils upon their hearts from understanding it, and a deafness in their ears. And if you invite them to the guidance, they will never be guided." (Qur'an 18:57)

Whosoever continues to take partners with the Almighty, then the risk is a crime that God will not forgive:

"God does not forgive that partners be set up with Him, and He forgives other than that for whom He pleases. Whoever sets up partners with God has indeed invented a great sin." (Qur'an 4:48)

Are we not surprised that the complaint of our beloved Prophet Mohammed on Judgment Day will be:

"And the messenger said: 'My Lord, my people have deserted this Qur'an.'" (Qur'an 25:30)

We have deserted the Scripture by not believing in what it said; we have deserted the Scripture by not trusting in the eternal words of God and in taking other sources for our guidance... We have given ourselves and our minds over to others to read for us, explain for us, think for us and act as God for us.

Satan has entered the Muslims through their love for the Prophet and their desire to follow the command of God to "obey the Messenger." Is it not a fact that the Scripture contains the words of both God and His Messenger? Indeed, he who has accepted and followed the Scripture has accepted and followed both God and His Messenger.

> *"And when God Alone is mentioned, the hearts of those who do not believe in the Hereafter are filled with aversion; and when others are mentioned besides Him, they rejoice!" (Qur'an 39:45)*

After reading the above passage, ask yourself the following question: Can you stand to mention *God Alone*?

God does not forgive that partners be established with Him, but He forgives other than this... Reflect on what has been said and reflect on your very lives for it is your soul that is at stake. Read the Book of God as if you've never seen it before; read it with your eyes, ears and mind and reflect on every word that is being said to you. Take nothing for granted and do not allow anyone to make your decisions. For on the Day of days, you will be standing alone, and you will have to answer for your own deeds and your own choices.

We Must Change

The objective of this book has been to awaken the Muslim reader as to the core problems that have plagued our understanding of the system of Islam. The problems that have turned it from a vibrant and dynamic system that led the world and set the role model for justice and equality into a system of dogmatic practices and superstitious beliefs that spread ignorance and injustice.

The heart of this vibrant and dynamic system has always been the Scripture, which is the jewel in the crown and the beacon from heaven to lead us out of the darkness and into the light.

Upon comparing Islam as revealed by God and His Messenger to the "versions" being followed by up to 1.2 billion people, the differences are quite Earth-shattering:

- In Islam, the requirement to be a Muslim is to simply accept and live according to the "Straight Path" (6:151-153), vs. the Sunni or Shia five and ten pillars, which come from unauthorized books.

- In Islam, abolishing slavery is taught to be an act of righteousness (90:12-13), vs. Sunni and Shia teachings, which encourage slavery under war.

- In Islam, women are never forbidden from praying or fasting during menstruation (2:222) nor is there a specific dress code (i.e., the headscarf) imposed on them beyond modesty, vs. the Sunni and Shia which teach the undermining of women and forcing them to cover their hair and avoid praying or fasting at certain times.

- In Islam, a man or women may leave a will, after settlement of debt (4:12), vs. Sunnis who refuse to accept wills if there are any direct descendants.

- In Islam, monogamy is the basis for normal relationships, while polygamy is only allowed in cases involving a man marrying the mothers of orphans already under his guardianship (4:3), vs. Sunnis where a man may be a polygamist simply if he can afford to, and Shia which allow sex for pleasure (Mut'a).

- In Islam, divorce is enforceable only after an interim period, and it may be made nullified if the couple reconcile before the end of this period (65:1, 65:4), vs. Sunni teachings that destroy families by allowing a divorce to occur on the spot with no waiting period and no nullification.

- In Islam, thieves do not have their hands cut off but are detained and made to serve as a punishment for that which is stolen (12:76), vs. Sunni and Shia teachings which brutally amputate the hands causing disability.

- In Islam, adultery is not punishable by killing or stoning (24:2), vs. Sunni and Shia laws of stoning married adulterers to death.

- In Islam, absolute freedom of faith is allowed (2:256, 10:99, 18:29, 88:21-22), vs. Sunni and Shia requiring apostates to be killed and rejecting the practice of other faiths.

- In Islam, people are acknowledged as being diverse and each is to be respected for his/her level of spiritual growth (49:14), vs. Sunni and Shia teachings that all followers of their religion must think, act and even look the same (cult syndrome).

- In Islam, war can only be declared in cases of self-defense or to avert oppression (2:190), vs. Sunni and Shia teachings allowing raids and attacks on any people who are considered non-Muslim by their standards.

- In Islam, any person at any time can pray to God (2:186), vs. Sunni and Shia teaching that prayer can only be carried out at specific times and in a specific form.

- In Islam, Pilgrimage is a center for gathering of nations and for all to witness the benefits of the monotheistic form of government and from being together (22:27-28), vs. Sunni and Shia, which bring in polytheistic rituals and superstition (touching of black stone, circling seven times, etc.).

- In Islam, a year is a luni-solar count made of 365 days (17:12, 9:36), with all the seasons fitting in place, vs. the Sunni teaching that it is to be a lunar one based on 354 days, which creates confusion of seasons and time.

- In Islam, males and females are not required to be circumcised (32:7), vs. Sunni and Shia teachings requiring all males to be circumcised and females in some cases.

- In Islam, music, statues, gold, and silk are lawful (7:32-33, 16:116), vs. Sunni and Shia beliefs forbidding silk and gold for men while not allowing music and statues for anyone.

- In Islam, rule of government is under a constitution derived from the Book of God and by free speech (5:48, 42:38), vs. Sunni teachings allowing the rise of dictators or monarchs, and Shia teachings that uphold self-appointed religious leaders based on genealogy.

Therefore, the widest difference is that Islam is a monotheistic, clear, consistent, dynamic, progressive and balanced system. It is a system that eliminates conjectures, hearsay, fairy tales, contradictions, hardship, confusion, chaos, and division. Islam is a system that puts more accent on the usage of intellect, reason, pondering over God, His Creation, meaning of life, and pondering over everything else. The sects, on the other hand, represent superstition, unfair treatment for non-cult members, inequality of the sexes, oppression of human rights, inability to contribute to human progress, amputations or physical violence, regression of ideas and thoughts to primitive levels of barbarism, and most importantly setting up partners with the One True God and thus promoting polytheism.

Now, the choice that we as Muslims face is a difficult one: Do we continue implementing and upholding the teachings of the sects that have proven their failure time and time again and that have taken our societies deeper into the abyss of hatred, corruption, oppression, inequality, injustice, and intolerance? Or, are we willing to take the path of God Alone and implement the ideal system contained within the pages of the Scripture?

What Can You Do?

Below are four steps that we ask the reader to undertake:

1. Verify What Has Been Said

This book has been written to promote a new dawn for Islam and a return back to the pure teachings of God and His messenger. If there is only one thing to be learned from this book, then that is the requirement that we should all *verify* every single piece of information we are given by taking nothing for granted.

> *"And do not uphold what you have no knowledge of. For the hearing, eyesight, and mind, all these you are responsible for." (Qur'an 17:36)*

2. Correct Your Mistakes

If you have verified the information and been witness to the verses that are quoted, then the next step is to change those aspects in your lives that are at contrast with the teachings of the Scripture. If you are expecting a newborn son, then do not circumcise him. If you are wearing the Hijab, then know that it is not required by God that you do so. If you are still performing rituals promoted by Hadith, then abandon them and wash yourself clean of all idolatry. Speak truth, help others, give charity, be humble, do not backbite, do not curse, do not commit lewdness… These are all the signs that a person has followed the light and beacon sent to us by God, by upholding them and becoming an example to humankind.

> "And whoever repents, and does good, then he shall repent towards God a true repentance. And those who do not bear false witness, and if they pass by vain talk they pass by with dignity. And those who when they are reminded of the revelations of their Lord, they do not fall on them deaf and blind. And those who say: 'Our Lord, grant us from our mates and our progeny what will be the comfort of our eyes, and make us leaders of the righteous.' These will be rewarded with a dwelling for what they have been patient for, and they will find in it a greeting and peace. In it they will abide, what an excellent abode and station." (Qur'an 25:71–76)

3. Advise Others

Spread the word of God to those around you beginning with your family and close circle and then extending outward (20:133). Do not remain silent when you see falsehood being carried out, or the words of God being twisted and lied about. Abraham has set the precedent for us when he confronted his peoples' misguided behavior and risked being thrown in the fire for his actions (6:80). However, remember that the ultimate guidance can only come from God; therefore you shall invite people to His path with kind words and good advice and never through harshness or force or intimidation, for these are not ways sanctioned by God.

"Invite to the path of your Lord with wisdom and good advice, and argue with them in that which is better. Your Lord is fully aware of who is misguided from His path, and He is fully aware of the guided ones." (Qur'an 16:125)

"It was a mercy from God that you were soft towards them; had you been harsh and mean hearted, they would have dispersed from you; so pardon them and ask forgiveness for them, and consult them in the matter; but when you are convinced, then put your trust in God; for God loves those who put their trust." (Qur'an 3:159)

4. Promote Implementation of the System of God

The path of monotheism is through peaceful and open debate. It is a path of non-violence. The Scripture only permits fighting when attacked or aggressed against and never is it permitted as a political vehicle to bring change by force. Educate yourself to the merits of the system of life and government in the Scripture and begin to lobby for its implementation. Show people how their rights would be protected, how their taxes would be limited, how their needs would be represented, and how law within such a constitution would ensure their freedoms.

"He is the One who sent His messenger with the guidance and the system of truth, so that it will expose all other systems, even if the polytheists hate it. 'O you who believe, shall I lead you to a trade that will save you from a painful retribution? That you believe in God and His messenger and strive in the cause of God with your money and your lives. This is best for you, if only you knew.'" (Qur'an 61:9–11)

It is not too late...

Gone are the days of dictators and kings and corrupt leaders and burying infant girls in the sand... Gone are the days of lying about God and His Messenger by inventing laws and rules and regulations in their name...

We can still work to correct what has gone wrong with our societies and to prosper–like the people of Jonah did–in this world and the next:

> *"If there was any town that benefited from its belief, then that would be the people of Jonah. When they believed, We removed from them the retribution of disgrace in this worldly life, and We let them enjoy until a time." (Qur'an 10:98)*

But remember... God does not change anything unless we make the first step:

> *"That is because God was not to change any blessing He bestowed upon a people, unless they change what is in themselves. God is Hearer, Knowledgeable." (Qur'an 8:53)*

We are calling people back to the Qur'an.
We are calling people back to the true teachings of Islam.
We are calling people back to the path of God Alone.

For further information, please refer to the websites:

www.free-minds.org
www.brainbowpress.com
www.progressivemuslims.org
Or e-mail to free@free-minds.org

LaVergne, TN USA
05 September 2010
195936LV00001B/31/P